TRANQUILITY PARENTING

TRANQUILITY PARENTING

A Guide to Staying Calm, Mindful, and Engaged

Brittany Polat

ROWMAN & LITTLEFIELD
Lanham • Boulder • New York • London

Published by Rowman & Littlefield
An imprint of The Rowman & Littlefield Publishing Group, Inc.
4501 Forbes Boulevard, Suite 200, Lanham, Maryland 20706
www.rowman.com

6 Tinworth Street, London SE11 5AL, United Kingdom

British Library Cataloguing in Publication Information Available

Library of Congress Cataloging-in-Publication Data

Names: Polat, Brittany, 1983- author.
Title: Tranquility parenting : a guide to staying calm, mindful, and engaged / Brittany Polat.
Description: Lanham : Rowman & Littlefield Publishers, [2019] | Includes bibliographical references and index.
Identifiers: LCCN 2018027990 (print) | LCCN 2018036822 (ebook) | ISBN 9781538112434 (electronic) | ISBN 9781538112427 (cloth : alk. paper)
Subjects: LCSH: Parenting. | Parent and child.
Classification: LCC HQ755.8 (ebook) | LCC HQ755.8 .P635 2018 (print) | DDC 306.874—dc23
LC record available at https://lccn.loc.gov/2018027990

♾ ™ The paper used in this publication meets the minimum requirements of American National Standard for Information Sciences Permanence of Paper for Printed Library Materials, ANSI/NISO Z39.48-1992.

Printed in the United States of America

To my wonderful children—may you always know the path to happiness.

CONTENTS

INTRODUCTION

I was standing in the kitchen, slicing cucumbers for dinner, when I heard a crash. Then a whine, then a cry, then three little voices yelling at once: "Mommy! James[1] pulled my hair!" "Clementine took my car!" "Freddy knocked over our tower!" I smiled to myself. *Ah, kids!* I thought as I set down my knife and went to the living room to check on them. *They still have a lot to learn.* As I listened to three different accounts of how the tower had gotten knocked over, I reminded myself that I'm there to teach them how to get along, not to get angry at them for their imperfections. We calmly talked about what needed to happen next and what the consequences would be if they didn't follow directions. Within a few minutes we had smoothed things over, and they settled down cheerfully with their toys.

As I headed back to the kitchen, I thought back to the year before, when I had never heard of Stoicism. Before I became a Stoic, I would have responded to their pre-dinner disruption with annoyance, frustration, and self-pity. If I heard a crash, I came running from the kitchen, sure that something terrible had happened and we would be heading to the emergency room. If I heard a whine, I snapped at them impatiently and then felt guilty for losing my temper. If they snatched or argued or didn't share, I envisioned future criminal delinquencies and felt that their flaws were all my fault. After all, I reasoned, as their parent, I'm responsible for them. Shouldn't I be able to control their actions? What am I doing wrong?

But on that evening, as I went back to chopping vegetables, I didn't feel the least bit guilty or upset. I didn't blame myself or my kids for their little altercation. I didn't start thinking about all their flaws or my own failings as a parent. Instead I felt . . . calm. Accepting. At peace. Confident that I could deal with any challenges that arose. I was fully aware that my children and I are not perfect and never will be. But I was also aware that I have a choice about what to think and how to act when things get difficult. This is what Stoicism is all about: learning to think clearly and make good judgments about the most important things in life.

After I discovered Stoicism, and after I had practiced making Stoic judgments in my parenting, I found that I began to enjoy life more. Not only was I more patient and mentally relaxed, but I felt more alert and engaged than I had in a long time. I had the same life, the same kids, and the same circumstances, but a completely different way of looking at things. And on top of everything else, I was actually happy! It was almost unbelievable.

Well, I thought to myself as I finished the cucumber and started on the tomatoes, *maybe I should write a book about Stoic parenting. Stoicism has helped me so much, and I'm pretty sure I'm not the only one who thinks raising kids is stressful.* Suddenly I smelled something burning. The rice! The smoke alarm started chirping loudly and I turned on the noisy kitchen vent, trying to fan away the smoke and salvage what I could of the rice still crackling in the pan. The kids all ran into the kitchen, jumping and shouting excitedly. As I stood on a chair in the middle of the kitchen, trying to silence the alarm and the kids, I started laughing. What a disaster! *At least now I know how to handle things,* I told myself as I shooed the kids out of the kitchen and scraped the blackened bits out of the pan. I may never be a great cook, but at least I can be a Stoic. I can forgive myself for burning dinner and remind my family that they don't need perfect risotto in order to live a good life. All they need is a little wisdom, courage, and self-control, and they can make the best of everything that comes along.

At this point you might be wondering what Stoicism is, and how on earth it could be related to tranquility parenting. Before I tell you what Stoicism is, I want to tell you what it most definitely is not. Have you ever heard the word "stoic" used in everyday conversation? As in someone who doesn't show or even feel any emotion, or someone who is aloof and remote from other people? Please forget that definition immediately. That is how the word has come down to us over the centuries, but in reality this stony-faced and emotionless image couldn't be further from the truth. Real-life Stoics do value emotional tranquility in tough situations, and real-life Stoics do try to root out negative emotions such as anger, envy, and fear. But Stoicism is not about getting rid of all emotions, and it most certainly is not about disengaging from the world or other people.

So let me tell you a bit about what Stoicism actually is. Stoicism is a vibrant, practical, and very relevant wisdom tradition that teaches people how to be happy in any situation that life might throw at them. It was founded more than two thousand years ago as a school of philosophy in ancient Greece. Back then, studying philosophy meant something different from what it usually means today. It wasn't just about sitting around reading obscure books that no one could understand. It was much more practical and focused on how to be a good person and live a good life. Many competing schools of philosophy tried to explain how to live a good life, and Stoicism was one of the most prominent and respected of these schools. Some schools, like the Epicureans, thought that pleasure was the most important thing in life; others, like the Skeptics, suggested that you can't really be sure about anything. One group, the Cynics, even thought you should give up all your worldly possessions in order to be happy. And what did the Stoics say?

From the beginning, the Stoics have said that the only way to live a flourishing life is to focus on being a good person. The Greeks even had a special word for a flourishing, fulfilling, happy life: *eudaimonia*. Our English word "happiness" doesn't even come close to capturing the full meaning of this ancient idea. Achieving *eudaimonia* means you are happy, but not in the same way that you feel happy when you get a promotion at work or eat an ice-cream sundae. *Eudaimonia* is a stable condition, not a temporary feeling, so it doesn't come and go depending on what happens to you. The only way to find this lasting peace and happiness is to not worry about external things and to instead focus on living wisely.

OK, you might think, that sounds nice, but how is anyone supposed to actually do that? How does that apply to real life, and how does that apply to being a great parent? Fortunately, the Stoics were master psychologists, and they provided a lot of practical advice about how to practice moral excellence and find *eudaimonia*. In real life, today's Stoics use their reasoning ability to cultivate healthy, positive emotions (such as tranquility, contentment, and confidence) while trying to overcome negative emotions. Real Stoics value social engagement and work hard to be kind, generous, and fair to others. They don't just throw up their hands when they see a problem and say, "There's nothing I can do about it!" Instead, they roll up their sleeves and do as much as they can, while understanding that there are some things they just don't have the power to fix. Stoics appreciate the beauty of the world around them and understand their place in the grand scheme of things. Stoics know they can have a meaningful and happy life, no matter what life might bring.

Does that sound like something you'd be interested in? If so, I hope you'll keep reading, even if you're still skeptical about how Stoicism could actually make you a calm and mindful parent. I admit, I myself was pretty skeptical when I first heard about it. But I was at my wits' end and desperate enough to try anything. It was a difficult time in my life: I had just had my third baby, left a career I loved to become a stay-at-home mom, and felt that everything in my life was out of control. I didn't have any friends or family in our new town. I had insomnia and couldn't sleep at night, so I was exhausted all day. I was really a mess. And worst of all, I felt incredibly guilty about everything, that somehow it was all my fault. I didn't know where to turn or what to do, but I knew I needed to find wisdom somewhere.

I went online and typed in "books about wisdom." Several clicks later I ended up reading reviews of a book by William Irvine called *A Guide to the Good Life: The Ancient Art of Stoic Joy*. [2] Stoic joy? Hmm, I thought, that sounds unlikely but intriguing. *Click, click*. Next I saw Donald Robertson's *Stoicism and the Art of Happiness*. [3] What, more Stoicism and more happiness? Then I found *The Daily Stoic: 366 Meditations on Wisdom, Perseverance, and the Art of Living* [4] by Ryan Holiday and Stephen Hanselman. Wisdom, happiness, the good life, the art of living—OK, I figured, there must really be something here. A few more clicks and I'd begun my journey into Stoicism. Amazing but true: For the first time in history, I'd found wisdom on the Internet.

And I'm not alone in finding Stoicism to be incredibly useful. Even though it went underground for a long time after the fall of ancient Rome, the great Stoic authors (Seneca, Epictetus, and Marcus Aurelius) continued to be read and admired during the Middle Ages, Renaissance, and up to the present day. The philosophy has reemerged in the twenty-first century, and (thanks again to the Internet!) people from all over the world can connect and talk about how to apply Stoicism to modern living. There are Stoic doctors, teachers, police officers, pilots, mayors, and, of course, parents. Literally anyone can benefit from learning about and practicing Stoicism. (Did I mention that the Stoic philosopher Marcus Aurelius was also the Roman emperor? And Epictetus, the most brilliant Stoic teacher of all time, was a former slave.)

But this book is not about Stoicism per se. It's about tranquility parenting—in other words, how to apply the principles of Stoicism to parenting in our modern world. I will be referring to Stoicism a lot throughout this book, but with a special focus on how you can use it specifically as a caregiver to your child. In chapter 1 we will introduce tranquility parenting as a parenting philosophy that can guide you through the momentous task of raising a child. Chapters 2–8 will then show you how to apply this philosophy to stay calm, eliminate negative emotions, and help your child flourish. Chapter 9 will summarize some of the practical techniques we have discussed so that you can refer to them quickly when you need them. And in chapter 10 we will walk through step-by-step guidance for resolving tricky issues from a tranquility parenting perspective.

Who is this book for? It's for any parent who has ever worried about his child, lost her temper, or wondered if she was guiding her son or daughter toward a good life. In other words, it's for everyone! I can't promise you all the answers, but with Stoic philosophy as our guide, I will show you how to start finding out the answers for yourself. Many of the challenges and examples I use in the book relate to young children, because at the time of writing my kids are all age five or younger. However, the principles behind tranquility parenting apply to children of all ages. With some minor adjustments, you can adapt these concepts to fit a wide variety of kids and situations. That's the wonderful thing about basing your parenting philosophy on an *actual* philosophy—it can work for pretty much everyone. Whatever your situation, I hope you find that the basic principles behind tranquility parenting work for you.

I

Finding Tranquility

I

DEVELOPING A PARENTING PHILOSOPHY

Let's start with the basics. What is tranquility, and why should you want it as a parent? You might think of tranquility as the type of peace and calm you get when you retreat to an isolated mountaintop or deserted island: quiet, beautiful, contemplative, nothing around to bother you. As a busy parent with many demands on my time, I certainly find myself longing for a break like this sometimes. But we all know it's not realistic to expect this type of tranquility in our daily lives. Anyway, taking a nice vacation probably wouldn't make you a better parent in the long run!

No, the type of tranquility I have in mind is different. This tranquility is possible anywhere and in any situation, and you can create it for yourself with a little knowledge and practice. And this kind of tranquility will definitely help you become a better parent because it results from a wise understanding of life. This is the tranquility promised by Stoic philosophy, and this is the basis of the tranquility parenting approach you are reading about now.

But tranquility doesn't come from nowhere. It needs a deeply rooted source. That source is your own reasoning ability, which can tell you what is most important in life. When you become a parent, you suddenly have a double responsibility: You want to live your own life well, and you also want to help your child live well. So how do you decide what is important as a parent and as a person? How do you know what to do with your child? These are very big and possibly complicated questions.

But if your goal is to be a calm, mindful, and engaged parent, these questions need to be answered. There's really no shortcut to tranquility.

Most of us have the impression that we already know what is good in life. We have some sort of idea about what we should do and how we should live. Even if you've never sat down and thought clearly about what your core beliefs are, you certainly have them. Your decisions about what job or career path to pursue, where to live, and even what to have for dinner tonight are all the result of thoughts and actions on your part. (Maybe you did not directly choose some of these things, but you did choose how to react when these things happened to you.) You also decide, maybe subconsciously, how to approach parenting. Everything you think, do, and say is a result of your perspective on life and what matters most to you.

The modern Stoic William Irvine suggests that if we do not think clearly about our "philosophy of life," we run the risk of "misliving."[1] In other words, if we don't have a clear goal or purpose for what we are doing, we may just stumble along, making incorrect assumptions and reacting badly to things that happen to us. Another modern writer, Massimo Pigliucci, compares living without a philosophy of life to walking at night through a dark forest.[2] Without a guide, you will bump into things, trip over stones, fall in the mud, and probably not be any closer to your goal.

That is exactly how I felt after my youngest child was born. With three small children at home, I felt like I had completely lost my sense of direction. I didn't know how to raise kids. I loved my children with all my heart and wanted to be the best mother I could for them, but I always felt like my best wasn't good enough. My identity as a competent and capable adult was shattered. I had an image in my head of myself floating alone at night on a dark sea, drifting, unanchored, out into the void.

When I learned about Stoicism, I knew I had found what I was looking for. Instead of stumbling blindly down a dark path, I suddenly had a compass for moving in the right direction. I felt like I was no longer on my own. I might not always get things right, but with the wisdom of the ages to guide me, I can at least be confident that I know which way to go.

Stoicism helps us answer big and small questions about life by teaching us how to think clearly. That's really what the whole "philosophy of life" thing is about: learning how to think clearly about things. Once you understand which questions to ask, and how to answer those questions properly, you will have a clearer sense of what to do as a person and as a parent. For example, how should I *be* as a parent? How should I act and interact with my child? How does being a parent fit in with the rest of my life (relationships, work, personal interests, etc.)? We already know that our children are important, and that trying to be a good parent is one of the most important things we can ever do. But without a clear answer to these questions, we might end up "misparenting," or not parenting to the best of our ability.

So let's start asking questions. In this chapter we will first look at your core beliefs and how these contribute to your parenting philosophy. Then we will look at how these big-picture ideas can inform your priorities as a parent, as well as your everyday parenting decisions. I strongly believe that your core beliefs about life and your core beliefs about parenting are inseparable. How could someone believe one thing about the purpose of life but teach his or her child something else? Your child learns much about life just by watching you live it. Like it or not, you are teaching your child about your beliefs and priorities through your daily actions—which means it is really important to clarify what those beliefs and priorities actually are.

DEFINING YOUR CORE BELIEFS

Whether you know it or not, you probably have some core beliefs about life and parenting. For example, what are the important things in life that you devote your time and energy to? How do you treat the people around you? How do you respond to difficulties? These questions all relate to our core beliefs. One way to answer these questions is simply to skate by without really thinking about them: We can react to situations as they arise and try to make it through each day on autopilot. The problem is that it's very difficult to make good, consistent decisions on the fly, even if you have great intentions. A better approach is to sit down and think about what your beliefs are as a parent. If you're like me, you've always tried to be a good parent, but maybe you've never taken time to define exactly what that means. When you do start to think carefully about it, it becomes a very fuzzy concept. What does a good parent do? What are her qualities and characteristics? How does she make decisions?

Let's say you are in the checkout line at the grocery store and your daughter begs you to buy her favorite candy. (Because of course her favorite chocolate bar is right at her eye level while you are standing there waiting.) Are you a good parent if you buy her the candy? Or are you a good parent if you say no? At first it seems like such a simple decision; but when you start looking at it closely, it becomes much more complex. And the decision probably requires lots of background knowledge about your daughter and the situation. Has she already had candy today? Have you been running errands all day and she is really hungry? Are you about to eat dinner when you get home? Did she do something extra good and you promised her a treat?

In order to make this decision you will probably refer (subconsciously) to your core beliefs about parenting, whatever they may be. If you think your child deserves a reward for good behavior, maybe you buy the chocolate bar. If you want to teach patience and self-control, maybe you don't buy it. Or maybe you're embarrassed because she's causing a scene, so you buy the chocolate to keep her quiet. Whatever decision you make, ultimately it comes down to what you think is important in life: rewarding good behavior, teaching self-control, or not being embarrassed in the store.

The point is, even the simplest decisions may not be so simple when it comes to kids. And we make dozens, even hundreds, of these decisions every day. Most of our choices are split-second, and our reasoning happens in an instant. This is part of what makes parenting so stressful. Not only are you dealing with irrational little people and difficult situations, but you also are responsible for continuously making good decisions about everything. Constantly. It's mentally and emotionally tiring. And once decision fatigue sets in—usually right before dinnertime—you just want to tune out and not deal with it any more. This is probably when you start snapping at your kids, yelling at your spouse, and saying, "Let's just order a pizza tonight." Not that there's anything wrong with pizza.

Your decision-making process will be faster, easier, and less stressful if you already know what your basic beliefs are. If you can refer to an existing system of wisdom, you don't have to feel guilty about denying (or buying) your daughter the candy bar. You're just doing what you've already decided is right. It also means much less back-and-forth with your daughter about the whole thing because the decision has already been made. (Of course enforcing it is a separate challenge!) That means it's completely worth it to reflect on your parenting principles and priorities before you even need to make a decision. It will save you a lot of time and trouble down the road, especially in the middle of difficult situations.

How exactly do you decide on these parenting principles and priorities? After you decide on your core beliefs as a person, your core beliefs as a parent will naturally follow. You may already have a very clear idea about what your core principles are, or you may have no idea. Whatever your situation, some key concepts from Stoicism can help you define and clarify your philosophy of life and parenting.

THINKING CLEARLY AND DEALING WITH EMOTIONS

One of my favorite things about Stoicism is that it teaches you how to think clearly. It also provides a rationale for thinking clearly: Reason is our special function as human beings. No other creatures on Earth have our capacity for rational thinking, so it is both our privilege and our responsibility to use our reasoning ability well. The ancient Stoics called this "living in accordance with nature." We use our capacity for reasoning in order to live in harmony with the natural world, with other people, and with our own inner nature. As a result of this clear reasoning, we can understand how to live wisely and ultimately find true happiness and meaning in life.

I don't know about you, but I find this perspective on life very beautiful. I don't want to just muddle through life. As a parent, I probably don't want to just go with whatever seems best at the moment, which could cause confusion and inconsistency. Instead I want a clear, consistent, and beneficial strategy for dealing with my kids and being the best parent I can be. So it makes sense that I should devote some time to thinking clearly and objectively about my goals and priorities.

But before we start thinking clearly, there's another issue we need to talk about: emotion. Stoics in the past have been criticized for being "emotionless" or for wanting to get rid of emotions. This is not true at all! However, there is a reason for this misunderstanding. It's because the ancient Stoics always talked about eliminating "passions." But they used the word "passion" differently from the way we use it in English today. In the ancient Stoic sense, passion meant a strong, uncontrollable, and often negative emotion, such as anger, fear, greed, and envy. The Stoics said that you can't ever be happy or peaceful if you allow these negative emotions to take you over. No one makes good decisions when they are angry or jealous or afraid. So we should work hard to root out the negative passions. (We will talk more in later chapters about how to do this.)

On the other hand, there are many positive types of emotion that we should keep and even try to strengthen. For example, we can cultivate joy, gratitude, wonder, benevolence, love, and caring for others. Learning to think clearly about the world can help us overcome negative feelings and enhance positive ones. We can actually develop a deeper love for our families and become more cheerful and generous.

In fact, Stoics say there is no clear distinction between rationality and emotion. This is very different from the popular conception of emotion today, which holds that our emotions are separate from our reason. It's easy to understand why many people believe reason and emotion are separate. Often when we experience a strong emotion, it feels like a different, primal part of us is taking over. For instance, think back to the last time you were really angry. Do you remember the tension in your whole body, the cloud over your mind, the feeling that your blood was boiling? When you experience a strong negative passion, it can feel as though your thoughts and actions are totally beyond your control. Stoicism says this is not actually true.

Stoics say that if we dig deep enough, our emotions result from our beliefs about what is right and wrong. In order for you to get angry, you have to believe that someone has done something bad to you. If you think you have just been insulted, you will automatically feel angry. But if you don't feel insulted, you won't feel angry, because there's nothing to feel angry about. Your emotion (anger) followed from your belief that you were wronged. If you change your belief that you were insulted, you can also change your anger. It's simple cause and effect.

Part of learning to think clearly is understanding how your beliefs impact your feelings. This requires a lot of practice, and we will be talking about it throughout this book. For now, I just want to emphasize that our goal is not to eliminate all emotions but to reduce those negative emotions that can cloud your judgment and behavior. (Some types of emotions are healthy and necessary, and of course we want to keep those!) Once you learn how to reason properly, you understand that some things, like a whiny child, are not worth getting upset about. And in order to learn this, we need to talk about the heart of Stoic philosophy: wisdom and virtue.

WISDOM AND VIRTUE

Yes, you read that right. Wisdom and virtue are the keys to flourishing, happiness, and good parenting. I know you're probably thinking, *Really? Are we in the 1800s?* Wisdom and virtue sound very dull and old-fashioned, and not relevant for modern parenting at all. That's what I thought at first too. But if you'll just bear with me for a little while and give this idea a chance, you will see that it is very relevant to being a parent in the twenty-first century. So let's spend some time talking about how the Stoic perspective on virtue can help us define our priorities as parents and achieve tranquility.

As unpromising as it might sound, virtue is really the foundation of everything else we will be talking about in this book. Stoic virtue has none of the prudish connotations from the time of your grandmother's generation—it doesn't mean sitting at home knitting instead of going out and having fun. In this context, virtue is the pinnacle of human achievement. It means excellence of mind and spirit, especially in the face of great difficulties. Virtue is an "expertise or skill, the knowledge of how to live well in every way, which shapes the whole personality."3

People who are truly virtuous are kind, generous, helpful, passionate about important things, grateful for what they have, and understanding about the ways of the world. They know there are some things in life they can and should change, but there are other things they cannot change. Virtuous people have a sense of proportion about life. They are confident but not arrogant, sociable but not needy, bold when necessary and agreeable when it's more appropriate. Doesn't this sound like someone you want to be? And someone who would be a great parent?

We're not going to pretend that anyone is perfect. The ideal of the truly virtuous person is more of a model for us to strive for than anything we can actually achieve. It's certainly not meant to make you feel bad about yourself. On the contrary, thinking about virtue can help us understand what our priorities in life should be. If the truly excellent person I just described sounds like someone you would want to be (in a perfect world), then you can work toward that goal—even knowing you will never be perfect.

Fortunately for us, the Stoics don't just hold up an ideal and say, "Here it is. Good luck with that." They actually provide detailed instructions and advice on how to work toward true excellence. The most straightforward way is to look at virtue as having four main parts: wisdom, courage, justice, and self-control. These separate virtues are really just different aspects of one larger theme called virtue. As we live our everyday lives, it is helpful to think about these four different faces of virtue, because they help guide our actions in different situations.

Wisdom is the primary virtue. At a basic level, it simply means "understanding how to act and feel correctly."[4] Remember what we discussed above about thinking clearly? That's really what wisdom is. It's making correct judgments about the world based on clear knowledge of the way things are. Courage is applying wisdom to frightening or fearful situations. Self-control is applying wisdom to temptations and desires. Justice is applying wisdom "in our relationships with other people, at individual, family, or communal level, and knowing how to act generously and with positive benevolence, with friendship and affection."[5] Being a Stoic really means learning how to correctly understand and judge every situation you might encounter in life.

This concept of correct judgment can help us set guidelines and priorities for ourselves as parents. That's because the Stoics didn't just say that virtue is a great thing to have—they said that virtue is the *only* thing you need to be happy and fulfilled. You can flourish as a human being if you are virtuous. Period. Regardless of what else happens to you, you can maintain inner tranquility and happiness if you have true virtue. No matter what your child does, no matter what your partner does, no matter what happens at work or in the national news, you can still be happy. In other words, virtue is both necessary and sufficient for living a flourishing life.

As I said at the beginning of the chapter, tranquility doesn't come from nowhere. You can't just skim along the surface of life and expect to have a deep and lasting joy. Especially once you become a parent, you need to have deep roots to support both yourself and your child. It might be a little difficult at first, but it will pay big dividends later. And all good things in life are worth working for, right?

PREFERRED INDIFFERENTS

If virtue is the only thing that can make you happy, what about everything else in life? Should you sell all your worldly possessions and move to a hut in the woods? Of course not. Even if virtue is what ultimately leads to flourishing, we can still make use of other things in life. In fact, Stoics have a special term for everything that is external and not related to virtue: "indifferents." If something does not help you achieve moral excellence, then it is indifferent. For example, cars, clothes, careers, and candy bars are all indifferents because they have nothing to do with personal virtue. You could do great things with fifty candy bars (donate them to a soup kitchen) or terrible things (eat them all yourself in one sitting). You could use money to help or hurt people. You can use popularity to do good or bad things. In other words, indifferents are just the raw material for people to act on. Things in themselves are not good or bad, but what people do with them can be good or bad.

Of course it's hard to be completely neutral about everything in life, and the Stoics have always acknowledged this. What about sickness, and pain, and poverty? Surely you couldn't say that sickness and health are just the same? No, you couldn't. Instead, most Stoics say that being healthy is a *preferred* indifferent and being sick is a *dispreferred* indifferent. Obviously, if you could choose, you would choose to be healthy rather than sick. You would likewise choose pleasure over pain, wealth over poverty. But many times in life you don't get to choose. So the Stoics say that even if you are sick, or in pain, or have no money, you can still live a good life because you can keep your virtue (your personal excellence). Maybe it's not your choice to be ill, but that shouldn't stop you from being a good person.

The idea of preferred and dispreferred indifferents is going to be very important for us in this book. As parents we experience many dispreferred indifferents, such as staying up all night with a new baby or dealing with a rebellious teenager. At the same time, children also give us many preferred indifferents, like the privilege of shaping a child into a wonderful young person. But even if we would prefer at any given moment not to have a grumpy or smart-alecky child, we can still practice our virtues of wisdom, justice, courage, and self-control. In fact, this is the time when we most need to practice the virtues. Life will always throw undesirable situations at you. But just because something undesirable happens does not mean you have to respond with anger or frustration. You can choose to handle the situation with dignity.

A TRANQUILITY PARENTING PHILOSOPHY

Let's recap what we've talked about so far. Stoicism can provide a framework for deciding what is important in life—in other words, for determining your core beliefs. From a Stoic perspective, those core beliefs include:

1. **Thinking clearly.** We should use our reasoning ability to hold correct judgments and reduce negative emotions.
2. **Acting wisely.** Only virtue leads to a flourishing and happy life. The four primary virtues are wisdom, justice, courage, and self-control.
3. **Dealing with indifferents.** External things are indifferent and are not necessary for a happy life. Still, a reasonable person will choose to pursue preferred indifferents (health, financial stability, happy children) and to avoid dispreferred indifferents (sickness, financial instability, unhappy children).

We can now adapt these core beliefs to describe a philosophy of tranquility parenting. Everyone is welcome to devise his or her own, and I strongly encourage you to think about how you might adapt these principles for your own situation. I have found the following principles to be useful:

1. **Thinking clearly.** We should use our reason to have consistent, coherent parenting principles that direct our behavior. We should learn to bypass negative emotions so that we can deal with challenges more effectively.
2. **Acting wisely.** We should apply the virtues in all our actions. When we interact with our child, we demonstrate the beliefs and behaviors we think are important.

3. **Dealing with indifferents.** There will always be some undesirable situations we have to confront as parents. The way we choose to deal with indifferent things is up to us.

This tranquility parenting philosophy is broad enough to cover almost all the situations you might face as a parent. On the one hand, that is good, because you can easily refer back to it in many circumstances. On the other hand, it might be nice to have some more concrete and specific guidelines for everyday situations. That's why the rest of this book is devoted to giving you concrete guidelines for applying these core beliefs. In the final section of this chapter, we will start looking at how to use this philosophy in real life to become calm and confident in difficult situations.

TRANQUILITY PARENTING IN ACTION

Let's think back to the checkout line scenario we described earlier. You are standing in a long line at the store and your daughter begs you to buy a candy bar. Now imagine you've had a long day at work, you stopped by the store to pick up something for dinner, and both you and your daughter are tired and hungry. You feel your frustration rising as your daughter starts asking more insistently. The people around you in line are rolling their eyes or glaring. How can our new parenting philosophy help us in this situation? We'll go through it step by step.

First, we need to use our reason and bypass negative emotions. This situation is only a problem if you see it as a problem. You can choose to stay calm. Just because your daughter is whiny does not mean you have to be angry or embarrassed. For example, you can choose to see it as just a normal part of life. You can't expect to have a perfect child, can you? If you expect to have a perfect child, you will always be disappointed and upset with her. But if you expect your child to be whiny sometimes, then now is one of those times. She is a child and she has a lot to learn. There is no reason to be upset about it.

Likewise, just because the other people in line scowl at you does not mean you have to be upset by their disapproval. If they are nice people, they will feel sympathy for you. If they are rude people, they will glare at you. But if they are rude, why do you care what they think of you? You don't care about the opinion of an unfriendly person, do you?

Remember that you are the adult in any situation with your child; you are also a reasonable and calm adult. You have been dealing with challenges your whole life, and you are equipped to deal with this one. And now you have an additional tool in your mental arsenal: a tranquility parenting philosophy that can guide your actions.

Second, think about the virtues you are aiming for: wisdom, courage, self-control, and justice. Which virtues apply in this situation? Wisdom, of course, because you need to refer to your core beliefs and priorities to make a good decision. Self-control, because you need to control your anger and frustration. Possibly courage, if you need to withstand the angry glares of fellow patrons in line. But perhaps most of all justice, for deciding how to relate to your daughter as she tests your patience. What is a fair way to deal with her?

Now let's go to the third principle: dealing with indifferents. The indifferent that caused this stand-off is a candy bar, so let's deal with that one first. You know your daughter is hungry, but you also know that a candy bar is bad for her health and will spoil her dinner. You also think it's beneficial if she learns to control her desire for candy. So you have three good reasons for not buying the candy bar and only one good reason for buying it. It looks like the answer should be no. But is there a way to stave off her hunger without buying the candy bar? Can you buy some pretzel sticks instead, or give her a few sips of your water or some chewing gum?

The other indifferent to deal with is the whole whiny situation. Clearly this is not something you would choose if you had any choice in the matter. But even though you shouldn't get upset, you still have to deal with the problem. If this is a rare moment of whininess for your daughter, maybe you should just overlook the whining. If whininess is a persistent problem, maybe you should make a big deal over it. Use your good judgment to decide what's best.

I am not here to tell you how to discipline your child. There are many reasonable approaches, and Stoicism does not provide a direct answer for discipline. Instead we will focus on laying the groundwork for positive interactions with your child. So while tranquility parenting does not tell you what to do when your child misbehaves, it does tell you how to stay calm and use your practical wisdom to make good decisions. If you know how to be peaceful and present as you deal with the candy bar situation, you will make a good decision. If you allow yourself to feel guilty, become agitated, and worry about other shoppers' opinions of you, you might make a decision that is not in your daughter's best interest.

Tranquility parenting is really about trying to make good decisions, and you do that by using specific psychological tools. Once you master these tools, you will have them ready to pull out during difficult situations. The parenting philosophy itself is one of those tools. When you are stressed and tired, you don't have to reinvent the wheel every time you make a decision. Instead you just think back to the guidelines you already have. That's when you can ask yourself how the current scenario fits into your parenting philosophy:

- What negative emotions do you need to reduce?
- What virtues do you need to apply here?
- What indifferents do you need to deal with?

Remember, eliminating negative emotions is not about suppressing your emotions. It's about making a correct judgment of the situation and, therefore, understanding that there is nothing to get upset about.

This may seem like a lot of thought processing to go through as you make quick decisions, but once you get the hang of it, it happens almost automatically. I just spent several pages describing what is really a split-second response. That's why it's important to take the time to think about your response *before* you ever need it. When you are in the middle of a difficult situation, you'll know exactly what to do, without having to agonize over your decision.

Another way to think of it is like driving a car. Do you remember when you first learned to drive? I remember being incredibly nervous the first time I got behind the wheel. I was worried I was going to crash at any moment, and I had to consciously focus on every little movement: Start the ignition, press the brake pedal, put the car in reverse, look in the rearview mirror, release the brake, change gears. But after practicing for a while, driving becomes second nature. After years of driving, you don't have to think about the background activities of steering the car. But you do have to stay alert and continually use your judgment, because other drivers are always doing unpredictable things.

You may know a road like the back of your hand, but you do not know if another car may come along and try to turn in front of you. You know the basic principles and skills of driving, but you always have to keep using your intelligence on the road.

Tranquility parenting is pretty much the same. In this book we are talking about the basic principles, and why you should adopt a philosophy of tranquility parenting. But it will take lots of practice to use and benefit from these principles. At first you may have to constantly refocus and be very deliberate in thinking through what you are doing. With time and practice, tranquility will become second nature, just like driving. You'll know just how to deploy your parenting philosophy, and you will be able to stay calm, think clearly, and make good decisions. I'm speaking from personal experience when I say that you really can do it. If I could go from being a stressed-out, anxious, unsure parent to one who is calm and confident, then literally anyone can do it.

With this basic philosophy, you can face any challenge. Of course you will always need to apply your practical reasoning to the situation, because every situation is slightly different. But I hope you're starting to see how Stoicism can help guide you toward tranquility. We've got a lot of ground to cover, but we will always come back to these core ideas: thinking clearly, acting wisely, and dealing with indifferents.

CHAPTER TAKEAWAYS

- If we don't think clearly about our philosophy of life, we risk "misliving." Similarly, if we don't think clearly about our parenting philosophy, we might "misparent," or act in a way that is inconsistent with our core beliefs. Our core beliefs should inform our parenting philosophy because our children start to develop their own philosophy of life by watching us.
- Stoicism can help us decide on a philosophy of living and parenting. Your everyday decision-making process will be faster, easier, and less stressful if you already know what your basic beliefs are.
- Emotion is not completely separate from reason. In fact, emotions arise from your beliefs about the world. If you change your beliefs, you can also change your emotions.

- Stoic virtue is excellence of mind and spirit, especially in the face of great difficulties. The four primary virtues are wisdom, justice, courage, and self-control.
- Virtue is the only thing you need to be happy and fulfilled. Regardless of what else happens to you, you can maintain inner tranquility and happiness if you have true virtue.
- External things (anything not related to virtue) are indifferents. Preferred indifferents are things we would like to have (good health, financial stability); dispreferred indifferents are things we don't want (sickness, poverty). Indifferents are not necessary for happiness and flourishing.
- Our tranquility parenting philosophy has three parts: (1) thinking clearly, (2) acting wisely, and (3) dealing with indifferents. You can apply this philosophy in any situation, although it may take time and practice to get used to it.
- Adopting a new parenting philosophy is like learning to drive a car. It takes a lot of thought and effort at first, but after a while it becomes second nature.

MAKE IT YOUR OWN

I strongly recommend taking some time to think about how you personally can apply tranquility parenting in your life. The Stoics always said that philosophy is not just about theory—it's about putting into practice what you've learned. If you want to get the most out of this book, sit down with a pen and paper and think it over for a while. Preparation is important. You will thank yourself later, when you're in the middle of a difficult situation! Here are a few things worth considering:

- What are your most important priorities as a parent? Does the philosophy described here fit with your priorities?
- Are there any particular situations that you find especially hard to deal with as a parent? If there are, imagine yourself applying this tranquility parenting philosophy the next time that situation arises. Remember all three parts: (1) thinking clearly, (2) acting wisely, and (3) dealing with indifferents.

- How can you practice virtue (personal excellence) in your daily life as a parent? For example, as you are going through the morning routine, picking up your child from school, or helping with homework?
- Our emotions result from our beliefs about what is right and wrong. Do you agree or disagree with that statement? If you agree, how do you think this knowledge can help you stay calm in difficult situations? If you disagree, please come back to this question after you have read chapters 2 and 3.

2

FOCUSING ON WHAT YOU CAN CONTROL

Can you control your child? Can you control what your child does? Can you control what happens to him, how other people treat him, or how things go in his life? The answer to all these questions, according to Stoic philosophy, is no. No matter how much you want to control your child and his life, you can't. It's logically impossible. It's *his* brain directing his actions, not *your* brain directing his actions. And when it comes to what happens *to* him, there is no way you can control what the rest of the world does.

But here's another set of questions. Can you influence your child? Yes. Do you have authority over him? Yes. Should you teach him to act wisely? Of course. Can you help him deal with difficult things that might happen to him? Definitely yes. These are all required of us as parents. We should proactively guide our children to become competent, ethical, and happy young people. This is the crucial distinction: We can influence, not control. If you try to control things that are not actually within your power, you will be frustrated, disappointed, and probably unhappy. On the other hand, if you keep in mind what you *can* control, and work within those bounds, you are much more likely to succeed in your goals. And you will probably also be calm and content, because you have done as much as you can to help your child become a good person.

In chapter 1 we clarified a philosophy of tranquility parenting, which includes thinking clearly, acting wisely, and dealing with indifferents. In this chapter we will put all these into practice by learning to focus on what we can control. If you have to choose just one thing to remember from this book, and even from all of Stoic philosophy, it should be this principle of control. It is the key to tranquility parenting. You might as well learn early on that you are not going to control your kids.

There will always be some things your kids do that, from your perspective, are frustrating, annoying, embarrassing, disappointing, or just plain wrong. I know it's incredibly difficult to step back from a given situation and realize that your child's behavior is not 100 percent up to you. But I have found that if you are able to truly internalize the dichotomy of control, you become not only a happier parent but also a better parent. So let's investigate how this dichotomy of control can have such a big impact on you and your family.

SOME THINGS ARE UP TO US, AND SOME THINGS ARE NOT

"Some things are within our power," said the great Stoic teacher Epictetus, "while others are not. Within our power are opinion, motivation, desire, aversion, and, in a word, whatever is of our own doing; not within our power are our body, our property, reputation, office, and, in a word, whatever is not of our own doing."[1] In other words, the only things in life we actually control are our own thoughts and actions. We don't control whether we get a certain job, or make a certain amount of money, or live a certain number of years (although of course we can take actions to try to influence these things). Even things that seem to be within our complete control, like getting up and going to work in the morning, are dependent on many other factors. You never know when something else could prevent you from reaching your goal. Maybe a tree fell on your car in the middle of the night. Maybe the subway is shut down. Maybe a hurricane is bearing down on your city. Maybe your company folded overnight. Even if you want to go to work, even if you try very hard to go to work, there is still a chance you won't make it. The point is, as we live our lives, so many things impact us that are not within our control.

Another thing that we don't control is our children. It's kind of difficult to accept when you first start thinking about it, because many of us have the impression that we are responsible for what our kids do. If your child misbehaves at school, you feel responsible for her misbehavior, even though you were not even there. Or if she's a perfect angel while playing with friends, you take credit for her good behavior, even though you weren't directly involved. It's kind of a paradox of modern parenting that even if we are not directly responsible for our children's actions, we still feel as though we're directly responsible. We seem to occupy a kind of ambiguous space of responsibility for our child's life, which leads to a lot of parental guilt and confusion. (Not to mention helicoptering.)

But remember, our goal in tranquility parenting is to think clearly about what we do as parents. We need to be absolutely certain about what is in our power to accomplish with our kids. If we spend our time and energy trying to do things that are impossible, we will always feel like a failure. Not because we are bad parents, but because we have set ourselves a task that is logically impossible: trying to control something that, by definition, you do not control. It's much more productive for you and your child if you focus on doing what is possible rather than doing what is impossible.

HOW MUCH DO YOU CONTROL YOUR CHILD?

To eliminate all confusion about how much control you have over your child, let's start by considering the person you have the most control over in life: a newborn baby. A tiny baby is completely dependent on your love and care for her very survival, so it's easy to think that you completely control her—that is, until you start trying to get her to do what you want. You want the baby to sleep? She'll only sleep if it's nap time and she isn't hungry or sick. You want the baby to play and laugh? You can make silly faces and tickle her all you want, but if she's not in the mood, she won't laugh. You want the baby to stop crying? I'm sure every parent has had the experience of desperately wanting his or her child to stop crying and not being able to make it happen. You try feeding, cuddling, swaddling, rocking, bouncing, singing, shushing, swinging, but nothing you do makes the crying stop. Yes, welcome to parenthood. You do not have control.

And if you don't control a tiny, helpless baby, think how much less direct control you have as your child gets older. For example, maybe your preschooler tries to snatch a toy from his friend and you tell him to wait his turn. That sounds straightforward. Well, let's consider two possible outcomes of this scenario. In the first outcome, you tell your son not to snatch, he listens to you, plays nicely, and waits his turn. Great! He's learned to control his impulses and wait patiently. But what if the outcome is different? Maybe after your intervention, your son snatches the toy again, his friend hits him, then they both start crying and screaming and struggling back and forth for the toy. Oops. Bad outcome.

In these two possible outcomes, you started with the same scenario, the same kids, and the same action on your part, but the result was completely different. What caused the different outcome? Maybe your son was tired and cranky, he was already upset about something else, the toy had his favorite cartoon character on it, or any other reason—or no reason at all. The point is, even with the exact same actions on your part, any given situation could have a totally different result. This is because you do not have 100 percent control over the situation or the children.

Think about a scenario from your own life. It could be getting your child to go to bed, practice the piano, clean her room, or be nice to her sister. No matter what it is, you do not have complete control over her. Sure, you can influence her using whatever tools you have available: reward, punishment, joking, persuading, coaxing, cajoling, or whatever else you think will work. You can use your knowledge and expertise to try to pick the right approach. But no matter what you do, you do not control your child's behavior—she does. Even if you were a perfect parent (which we know does not exist), and even if you did everything perfectly (which we know is impossible), you still would not control your daughter's decisions.

Even though we do not have complete control over our kids, we do still have responsibility, authority, and influence over them. Our actions certainly do impact their behavior. The way we respond to them on one occasion influences how they behave on the next occasion (and the one after that, and the one after that). That's the goal of instruction, correction, discipline, and guidance. So you could say that even though we don't have 100 percent control over our kids, we are still indirectly responsible for their actions.

This leaves us in an interesting position. If we do have responsibility, but don't have total control, then how should we approach raising kids? Clearly, we can't just sit back and do nothing. Even though we do not control our children, we are still committed to keeping them healthy, teaching them good behavior, and helping them reach their potential as they grow up. So how do we do that and still maintain our tranquility?

We will be answering that question throughout this book. For right now, let's come back to the Stoic dichotomy of control, which can help us decide what to focus on as parents.

AN UPDATED DICHOTOMY OF CONTROL

The dichotomy of control divides everything in life into two categories: "things I have complete control over," which are your own thoughts, feelings, and motivations, and "things I have no control over," which is everything else.[2] You can do your best to influence everything around you, including your child, but you cannot actually control these things. The modern Stoic author William Irvine suggests that instead of looking at only two categories, we add a third category, called "things I have *some* control over."[3] This category includes things that you do not completely control, but that you might be able to influence in some way. For example, I might not have complete control over whether I cook a delicious dinner, but I do have some control. There are steps I can take to increase the chance of dinner being delicious, like finding a good recipe, buying high-quality ingredients, and following the recipe to the best of my ability. But if something causes dinner to fail—I don't have the right size pan, or I have to deal with an emergency while I'm cooking—those factors are beyond my control. I may end up with another burned dinner, despite my best efforts.

Parenting is full of situations that you have some but not complete control over. If you want to get your child to school on time, there are certain things you can do to work toward this goal: Wake him up on time, get breakfast ready quickly, have everything packed and waiting by the door, etc. But you do not have complete control over getting him to school on time, because many things could happen to prevent you from getting there. Your child could wake up sick, you could get a flat tire on the way, a traffic accident might shut down the highway. So your goal of getting your child to school on time is partially dependent on you, but not completely dependent on you. You have some control, but not total control.

This category of "things I have some control over" is where most of our parenting frustrations take place. When you need to get something done, but it is not completely in your control, it's easy to start getting stressed out and annoyed. If you're trying to get your child to school on time and your three-year-old refuses to put his shoes on for no apparent reason, you are in the frustrating position of having responsibility (for getting him to school on time) but not control. If you want to have a peaceful family dinner but your kids break out into an argument, you might feel frustrated that you can't make your kids do what you want. When you want to control a situation but don't actually have control, you probably feel thwarted and disrespected.

So what is a parent to do? The trick is to focus on what you *can* control. What we *do* control completely are our goals, attitudes, and responses to the people around us. We can't dictate the outcome of a situation, but we can determine what we put into it. So let's go with that.

INTERNALIZING YOUR GOALS

You might not be able to control what your child does in any given situation, but you can control your own expectations for the situation. In his *Guide to the Good Life*, Irvine suggests shifting your goals from external to internal. Instead of your goal being *I will get my child to school on time*, your goal could be *I will do my best to get my child to school on time.*[4] In the first version, accomplishing the goal depends on your child and the rest of the world cooperating. That may not happen, and then you will have failed. But the second version depends only on yourself. Even if you get a flat tire on the way, you will still have accomplished your goal of doing your best to get there on time.

The distinction is subtle, but it makes a huge difference for your stress level. So often as parents, our goals for ourselves are actually dependent on our kids. If your goal is for your child to become a doctor when she grows up, accomplishing that goal does not depend on you—it depends on her. If your goal is for your child to use good manners at dinner, reaching that goal does not depend on you—it depends on him. If any of your goals depend in any way on other people, there is a very good chance you will be disappointed in some or all of them. You won't reach many of your goals, and you may feel like a failure.

The way to change that is to change your goal: *I will do my best to help my son be polite at the dinner table.* Accomplishing that goal does not depend on anyone except yourself. It is completely feasible and realistic. Even if your son doesn't use good manners at dinner, you can still accomplish your goal of *helping* him to use good manners. Mission accomplished. And maybe your reminders today will help him be more polite tomorrow.

There are many benefits to internalizing your goals in this way. First, you will feel like a much more successful parent because you are setting realistic goals for yourself. Second, you will actually be much more effective at parenting. Let's take the dinner table scenario. If you are focused all evening on an external goal—your child using good manners—you will feel frustrated whenever your son starts acting up (frustrated at him for not minding and frustrated at yourself for not being able to make him mind). You will be so focused on the outcome that you can't even enjoy your dinner. But if your goal is to *help* your son learn better manners, you will be focused on your own input to him. Instead of getting upset about his bad manners, you will be trying to deliver the best instructions you can.

Maintaining realistic expectations is an important component of staying calm. You see, if we have external goals that depend on our kids, our kids actually have all the power in the situation. If they refuse to cooperate, our goal is missed and our day ruined. And I'm pretty sure our kids can sense when we're desperate. If your happiness, or your identity as a good parent, depends on your child acting in a certain way, you're letting your child control you. That's a lot of power to hand over to a young child.

But if we keep our goals internal, we maintain our authority in the situation. You can reach your goal of being the best parent you can be, regardless of how your son behaves. You will never have your evening ruined by his misbehavior, and you will consistently work toward your goal of being a wise parent.

Keep in mind that this technique of internalizing goals is never an excuse not to try. You're not allowed to give up at the slightest obstacle and say, "Oh, well, I tried. Too bad it didn't happen." It doesn't work that way. You must be sure that you are holding up your end of the bargain, and if you're not actually doing your best, you haven't reached your goal. Tranquility parenting is never an excuse. It is a tool.

As long as you keep that caveat in mind, you can successfully internalize your goals in almost any situation. Instead of *making my daughter practice the piano*, change your goal to *helping my daughter practice the piano*. In the first scenario, your goal depends on your daughter's actions (she must practice the piano). In the second one, your goal depends on your own actions (you help her). Yes, of course your desired outcome is to get her to practice the piano. The tactics you use are probably going to be the same. But your outlook, and therefore your overall approach, will be different. You won't need to get frustrated or mad at anyone.

Internalizing goals works for both small, everyday problems and big-picture parenting issues. We've looked at how you can use this strategy in specific situations, such as being polite at the dinner table. But you can take the same approach with big goals, such as helping your child become academically successful or helping him become a giving person. You will have external strategies that you use to instruct, encourage, guide, and discipline. (We will talk more about these in chapters 4 and 5.) But your goal will be *helping* your child to become a giving person, not *making* your child a giving person. There is no way you can *make* him become a certain way, but you certainly can *help* him become a certain way. That small change in emphasis makes all the difference.

FOCUSING ON INPUT RATHER THAN OUTCOME

Another way of looking at the same problem is to focus on your own input into the situation rather than the outcome. You can control what you put in; you cannot control what you get out. The outcome depends on other people. No matter how excellent you are, no matter what you do, you might not get the results you wanted.

What kind of input do you have in any given situation? According to our original quote from Epictetus, we control our "opinion, motivation, desire, aversion, and, in a word, whatever is of our own doing." So that's it: opinion, motivation, desires, aversions, and actions. No matter what anyone else does, we contribute those five components to any interaction. And notice that the first four component don't even involve your actions toward your child—they are purely related to your own frame of mind. Before you take action, you should be sure your opinion and motivation are accurate and reasonable. Let's see what this would look like in a real-life scenario.

Imagine you have a teenager who spends too much time on her mobile phone. She stays up late texting her friends, she spends time on Snapchat instead of doing her homework, and she's gotten in trouble at school for using her phone in class. You're frustrated because you've already set limits and even threatened to take the phone away, but ultimately you feel that she needs to have a phone for safety reasons. You feel stuck. You don't want to eliminate the phone, but your daughter is making bad choices with the phone. What do you do?

Remember, before you make the actual decision about what action to take with your daughter, you should think about your opinion, motivation, desires, and aversions. Let's walk through all five elements and see where they lead.

Opinion. You control your opinion of the situation. Is this the worst thing that's ever happened? No. Are there plenty of other parents and teenagers going through exactly the same problem? Yes. Are you capable of making things better? Yes. OK; that means this is not something you need to get upset about. So the first thing you need to do is make sure you have a realistic assessment of the situation. This is not the end of the world, and it's something that you and your daughter can work on together. View it as an opportunity to help your daughter learn and grow.

Motivation. What is motivating you to act? Are you worried? Do you feel alarmed, disrespected, or threatened? Try to diagnose your own feelings, and then try to bypass those negative emotions. (We will talk more about how to do this in chapter 3.) In tranquility parenting, you always want to act out of a desire to teach, not punish. If your knee-jerk reaction is to get upset and yell at your daughter, try to step back and calm down before talking with her. Remember, your ultimate motivation is love and concern for your daughter.

Desires. What do you want to accomplish here? There are two general goals you could desire: fixing the immediate situation (short-term goal), or the larger picture of helping your daughter become a good person (long-term goal). Have you heard the expression *lose the battle but win the war*? I always keep this in mind when I'm frustrated with my kids. You might "lose" on a particular day if your daughter decides to make another bad choice. But is she a good kid? Does she make good choices in most other areas of her life? Is she usually responsible and courteous? Is she passionate about some things? Remember, everyone makes mistakes on the way to becoming a good person. As long as she is mostly getting things right, you are probably winning the war.

Aversions. Is there anything you are running away from here? Are you afraid of being a bad parent? Are you worried your daughter's grades will suffer and she won't get into a good college? Do you believe she will fall in with the wrong crowd and start participating in criminal activities? It's important to be honest with yourself. I think it's normal to have some underlying concerns like this, but you need to be aware of how they are influencing your decisions. Be sure your concerns are reasonable and valid. If you have a real basis for concern about your daughter's friends, then take appropriate action. Just try to think clearly about what you are doing and why you are doing it.

Actions. Now that you've thought through the situation carefully, you can make a good decision about what to do. By all means, do what you think is necessary to curb her cell phone use: Talk to her teachers, assign consequences, apply parental controls, allow her to use the phone only after homework is done, etc. There is no one-size-fits-all solution. You must be the judge of what is best for your daughter. Just remember that only *your* actions are your own doing; your daughter's actions are *her* own doing.

Focusing on your own input allows you to stay calm and keep things in perspective while you actively work toward solving the problem. There is no magic wand in parenting, and no guarantee that your daughter will suddenly start cooperating. But if you practice thinking clearly and acting wisely, you can at least be confident that you are doing your best to help your daughter. And at the end of the day, that's as much as you can do.

A MOVING TARGET

In this chapter we've talked about keeping your focus on what you can control. The ancient Stoics compared this way of handling problems to an archer shooting at a target. Just imagine you are standing with a bow and arrow in your hand, aiming at a target. You do your best to aim well. You take your time, line up the point of your arrow, hold the bow firm and steady, and then you let go. Now you no longer have control over where the arrow flies. There are many things that could prevent it from hitting the target: Wind could blow the arrow off course, the target could move, or something else could interfere. You don't actually control whether the arrow hits the target. You only control whether you aimed well.

Being a parent is similar to being an archer trying to hit a moving target. (Except our targets also turn somersaults, complain about dinner, and wet their pants.) You can have true aim, a steady hand, and lots of experience, but you still may not get the outcome you wanted. What do you do when that happens? Keep doing what you believe is right, and keep trying to think clearly and act wisely. Focus on controlling your arrow, not on what happens after you let the arrow go. Just try to keep your aim straight and true.

Just like a good lawyer can't win every case, a good doctor can't save every patient, and a good ball player can't win every game, a good parent can't resolve every situation in the way he or she would like. But what we can consistently do is play the game well. So even if external factors prevent you from "winning" that day, you can still be confident that you played well.

Your child will always throw surprises at you, and that is part of the beauty of parenting. We never know exactly how things will go from one day to the next. But what we can know for sure is that we are equipped to deal with the challenge, and privilege, of parenting. If you keep your focus on what you can actually control, you will always keep your cool. In the next chapter we will talk more about how to be calm and confident during some of those tough interactions with your child.

CHAPTER TAKEAWAYS

- The only things in life we completely control are our thoughts, feelings, attitudes, opinions, goals, and actions. Over everything else, we have only partial or no control.
- You do not have 100 percent control over your child. But you do have responsibility, authority, and influence, which you should use as wisely as possible.
- The trichotomy of control divides everything in life into three categories: things I have complete control over, things I have no control over, and things I have some control over. Many of our parenting frustrations take place in the last category: things I have some control over.
- To overcome your lack of control over your child, you can internalize your goals. Instead of having as your goal *I will get my child to school on time*, your goal can be *I will do my best to get my child to school on time*. You can internalize your goals in any parenting situation, big or small.
- Don't think that internalizing goals is an excuse for inaction. It is reframing, not giving up. You must still try your best, just in a different way.
- In any situation, focus on your own input, not the outcome. There are five things you can control when you interact with your child: your opinion, motivation, desires, aversions, and actions.
- Remember the metaphor of the archer: Focus on controlling your arrow, not on what happens after you let the arrow go. You can have true aim, a steady hand, and lots of experience, but you still may not get the outcome you wanted.
- No matter what happens, you can play the game well. Sometimes you might lose the battle but win the war—you might be dealing with a tough situation, but you are still raising a wonderful young person.

MAKE IT YOUR OWN

- Think carefully about what you can and cannot control in your life. You might want to make a list with three columns to represent the trichotomy of control: things I have complete control over, things I have no control over, and things I have some control over. In each column, write as many items as you can think of from your own life.

- Now think of your biggest frustrations as a parent. Under which column do they belong? Write them down. When you've encountered these frustrations in the past, have your goals been external or internal?

- Think about how you can internalize your goals for each of these frustrations. Write down your new goal beside each one. Imagine yourself encountering each frustration in real life and then applying your new internal goal.

- Choose your biggest parenting challenge. Now imagine yourself in that scenario focusing on your input rather than the outcome. Go through all five parts: opinion, motivation, desires, aversions, and whatever is of your own doing (action). This will help you be prepared the next time you run into a challenging situation.

3

RETHINKING YOUR VALUE JUDGMENTS

As we go through our daily routines as parents, we usually don't stop to think about whether our impressions of things are accurate. We are always so busy, and most of the time we are on autopilot: Wake up, get your child ready for the day, run errands, pay bills, fix dinner, etc. Things happen, and we deal with them as seems best to us at the time.

But as you now know, Stoicism teaches us that we shouldn't go through life on autopilot. If you want to be happy and fulfilled as a parent, you must really stop and think about what you are doing. That's what we've tried to do so far. In chapter 1 we described a parenting philosophy that prioritizes thinking clearly, acting wisely, and dealing with indifferents. In chapter 2 we discussed one very important component of thinking clearly: focusing on what you can control. In this chapter we are going to look at another aspect of clear thinking that will lower your stress level and help you deal with challenges more effectively.

Let's pause for a moment to consider how you make judgments about things in your life. We make judgments all the time, mostly unconsciously and without questioning them. If your child is doing well at school, that's good; if she's getting in trouble at school, that's bad. If you have dinner ready on time, that's good; if you burn dinner to a crisp, that's bad. This way of forming value judgments is a habit we acquire as we grow up and learn about the world. And of course judgments are necessary for survival: A lion chasing you is bad; a tree full of ripe fruit is good. There's a reason we see the world this way. But when we start to apply these good-or-bad judgments to things that are not actually good or bad, it can cause more harm than benefit.

For example, imagine that your toddler is in the middle of a big temper tantrum. Is this a bad thing? Well, of course it is a dispreferred indifferent, because no one wants to deal with a tantrumming toddler. We'd much rather have a happy toddler on our hands. But a tantrumming toddler is not an absolutely bad thing, because it is not related to your virtue. Does your toddler's tantrum make you a bad person? No. (Even though the people staring at you might think otherwise. Just ignore them.) Does your toddler's having a tantrum make you a good person? No. It's morally indifferent. It is neither morally good nor bad.

If you judge an indifferent situation to be good or bad, you are making an error of judgment. As a result, you will feel embarrassed, guilty, furious, and frustrated by a tantrumming toddler when there is no reason for you to feel bad at all. Did you do anything vicious to start the tantrum—did you steal, cheat, harm, neglect, or destroy? No, I didn't think so. More likely you just told your toddler that she couldn't have something she wanted. In that case, you are doing what you thought was right and trying to be a good parent. There is absolutely no reason for you to feel ashamed just because your virtuous act provoked an undesirable reaction.

If you apply a mistaken value judgment to the situation, your actions will probably be guided by negative emotions. If your toddler throws a tantrum in a store and you buy her candy just to quiet her down, you let your embarrassment dictate your actions. If you start to feel like you're a bad parent for letting this happen in the first place, your sense of guilt overwhelms your judgment. But if you stay calm and remember that this is just a dispreferred indifferent, you can keep your wits about you and deal more effectively with the problem. Remember to focus on what you can control. You may not be able to control all of your child's actions, but you can control your own. Once you learn to apply correct judgments, a lot of your stress and frustration evaporates. You are much closer to tranquility and can devote more energy to interacting positively with your kids.

So how do you form correct judgments? I'm so glad you asked. It all starts with thinking about how we interpret information from our environment and how we use that information as the basis of our own actions.

FIRST IMPRESSIONS

The ancient Stoics taught that the basic building blocks of our experience are impressions. We receive sensory information about the world around us, and we use it to form impressions about the way things are. But our impressions are based not just on objective external information. This sensory information is combined with our existing knowledge, expectations, and prior experience in a process that looks something like this:[1]

1. We perceive an external object or situation.
2. We interpret the event to ourselves by combining sensory information, prior experience, existing attitudes, etc.
3. We create a value judgment about the impression.

Most of the time this process seems immediate to us, and we don't think to question our impressions. But impressions can be deceptive. Sometimes, as in the case of reflexes, we really do have a "pure" impression based on sensory information. If you touch a hot stove, you immediately draw back in pain. There's not much time for additional processing. For most other impressions, though, there's a lot of additional mental processing that happens at the same time. This is where value judgments come in.

Value judgments are our interpretation of external objects and events and how they impact our own lives. We are not detached observers of life; we are active participants. When something happens to us, we try to figure out what the event means for our own ego and sense of self. For example, if you're driving down the road and someone cuts you off, you don't simply perceive that there is now a different car right in front of you. You probably feel mad that the driver was so rude, personally insulted that he thought he's better than you, and frustrated that you are now even farther back in traffic. That's what the value judgment is all about—not just what happens but how it impacts your own role in the world.

We use the same subconscious method of impression formation when we interact with our kids. If your child doesn't cooperate when you tell him to go to bed, you assign a value judgment to the situation. You might be thinking, "This is cutting into my alone time," or "If he doesn't get enough sleep, I'll have to deal with a cranky kid tomorrow." Or maybe even, "This is the tenth time he hasn't followed directions today! What is wrong with him?" Whatever it is you're thinking, you're not just objectively taking in information. You are interpreting it. Even if you judge something to be neutral, that in itself is a value judgment.

Let's break down the process again with a real-world example. Say I have two children arguing in the backseat of my car. Here's how my thought process might look:

1. **Perception:** I hear fighting; I look in the rearview mirror and see angry little faces.
2. **Interpretation:** My kids are fighting.
3. **Value judgment:** "Seriously? I have to deal with this again? We're already running late, I'm stressed out, and now my kids are yelling at each other. Ugh! What did I do to deserve this?"

Perception, interpretation, and value judgment. It all happens so quickly that we think it is one package. We mistakenly believe that our impressions are objective, when actually they include a value judgment that is very subjective. We tell ourselves that what we see is the truth, when actually it is our own interpretation.

Test out this theory for yourself over the next day or two. As you go through the day, think about how you are mentally processing and responding to events. If something unpleasant happens, do you jump to the conclusion that it is insulting or harmful for you? Do you feel angry and disrespected? I used to feel this way all the time. Whatever anyone did, I was quick to feel offended. If my husband didn't clear up his dishes after dinner, I felt he was personally insulting me. If I caught a red light when I was running late, I felt like the world was out to get me. If my kids didn't behave, I felt they were deliberately questioning my authority. It made me, and everyone around me, miserable. And as I now realize, it wasn't true at all. It was all based on false impressions.

REMOVING VALUE JUDGMENTS

So here's one of the great insights of Stoicism: Our usual subconscious method of forming impressions is inaccurate. If we want to see things as they truly are, we should remove the value judgment at the end of this thought process. That's because the value judgment is an opinion, not a truth. As the Stoic teacher Epictetus says, "It isn't the things themselves that disturb people, but the judgments that they form about them."[2] By removing an unnecessary and untrue opinion, you are unclouding your mind and enabling yourself to think about the situation much more clearly. You are actually bringing your perceptions of the world more in line with reality.

To demonstrate how this correction works, let's go back to the backseat bickering scenario. In our reformed thought process, the first two steps of forming an impression are the same. I still have the sensory information; I still form an interpretation based on my existing knowledge and experience. But instead of ending my thought with "Ugh! This is terrible," I just end with the basic interpretation that my kids are fighting. Now my impression looks like this:

1. **Perception:** I hear fighting; I look in the rearview mirror and see angry little faces.
2. **Interpretation:** My kids are fighting.

Voila! No negativity. Just the facts. It's not as though I'm trying to lie to myself or ignore reality. I still see the fight and know I have to deal with it. I am simply removing a value judgment that was not true in the first place. How do I know the value judgment wasn't true? Because by taking it away, my impression is no less true and no more false. My kids are fighting. That's it. Now I can deal effectively with my kids because I do not have negative emotions involved in the situation.

You might be asking yourself, "But aren't some things actually bad? Don't you need to keep negative judgments about some things?" The answer is yes. We are not talking about moral relativism here. If you see something bad happening, you should fix it. If your child misbehaves, you should correct and teach her. The part we want to remove is our sense of injury to ourselves.

Here is how the Stoic emperor Marcus Aurelius put it: "Say nothing more to yourself than what the first impressions report. You have been told that some person is speaking ill of you? That is what you have been told: As to the further point, that he has harmed you, that you have not been told."[3] You can objectively know that someone said something negative about you, but that does not mean you must get upset or feel offended. Your feeling of offense is not an objective truth. We are the ones who add that sense of insult and injury. And since we are the ones who put it there, we are the ones who can take it away.

When I see my kids fighting, I know that fighting is bad and that I need to correct them. But what I don't need is all the extra interpretation that says I'm a bad parent, or they're difficult kids, or this is the last straw on a hard day. Those are the kinds of value judgments we need to eliminate.

In tranquility parenting, I suggest that we replace value judgments with decisions and reactions. After you perceive an event and form an impression, you don't need the value judgment. But you do have to decide what to do, and then you have to do it. So here's what our improved thought process looks like:

1. **Perception:** I hear fighting; I look in the rearview mirror and see angry little faces.
2. **Interpretation:** My kids are fighting.
3. **Decision:** I need to correct my kids.
4. **Reaction:** I speak calmly but firmly to the children, and discipline as necessary.

See how it works? We don't need that layer of judgment in order to be effective. In fact, we can be much more effective without it. No need to think about how stressed out or frustrated you are, or how you've reached your limit with your kids. Just deal with the facts of the situation.

Let's look at a completely different example: You find out that your teenage son has been skipping class and lying about it. If you're not practicing tranquility parenting, your natural reaction is probably to become furious and start doling out punishment. You might feel betrayed, let down, and insulted: "I've loved him and done everything for him! How could he do such a thing to me!" You might feel sorry for yourself: "What did I do to deserve such treatment from my own child?" You might feel desperate: "I've done everything I know to do. What else can I possibly do to teach that boy?" These would all be normal reactions. But are they good reactions? Are they accurate; most of all, are they going to help anything? No, not really. They are just value judgments you are adding to your impression. Feeling desperate, incompetent, insulted, or enraged is not going to help you or your son in any way and will probably lead you to make bad decisions.

Instead of thinking about how likely your son is to turn into a juvenile delinquent, here's a different way of thinking about the situation:

1. **Perception:** You see his progress report or get a call from school about his absences.
2. **Interpretation:** Your son has been skipping class and lying about it.
3. **Decision:** This is a serious problem that needs your clear concentration, not your anger.
4. **Reaction:** You stay calm and figure out the best way to talk to your son, discipline as necessary, and provide guidance.

It's even more important for you to stay calm with an older child than with a younger one. Older children have more complex motivations for their behavior, plus they have more autonomy, and there are larger chunks of their lives that are not visible to you as the parent. Hopefully you are working toward a good relationship with your child, but even so, you won't always know what's driving him to behave in a certain way. By staying calm and keeping your ego out of the interaction, you can really make an effort to understand what is going on. You will need all your ingenuity to help solve the problem. You can still discipline him if you need to, but you will be disciplining out of love, not anger.

In chapter 1, I described how Stoicism is not about suppressing emotion but about removing your judgment that something bad is happening to you. This is how it works. It's not about trying to ignore your feelings or trying to be endlessly patient. Those strategies don't work (believe me, I've tried!). If you have an impression that something bad is happening to you, you are going to feel bad. And unfortunately, you can't bottle up your frustration and anger forever. If you try to keep being patient by ignoring your negative feelings, you will eventually crack. That's how you end up shouting at your kids and doing things you regret.

I like to think of it as an equation of mental energy. If you keep telling yourself, "I have to be patient with them, I have to be patient with them," all your mental energy is going toward being patient. In fact, so much of your mental energy is going toward being patient that you don't have much energy left for handling the problem. Or for enjoying your time with your kids. And since your mental energy is constantly getting used up, you will run out of it quickly and will constantly feel exhausted.

But if instead you recognize that you have not been harmed at all, then there's nothing to be patient about. You don't need to be patient because you're not angry or upset. Now your mental energy isn't draining out, and you conserve all your energy for more productive thoughts. You can focus your whole mind on solving the problem. And since you don't feel a sense of injury, you can enjoy being around your kids.

You might think I'm exaggerating the benefits of this mental technique. I'm not. At least, I've found it incredibly useful in my own parenting, and I encourage you to try it too. You might want to start by just noticing how often you make unnecessary value judgments, in all aspects of life but especially with your kids. Once you notice what you are doing, you can start to catch yourself before you do it. You can tell yourself that a value judgment is just an opinion, not a fact, so you can change or eliminate it. In fact, Epictetus advises us to actually treat value judgments like objects we can throw out. It might sound silly at first, but it's actually quite helpful to picture opinions like this. You could envision yourself crumpling up the false judgment and throwing it away. If that visual imagery doesn't appeal to you, you can always just remind yourself that you are in charge of your inner discourse, so it is within your power to change it. You control your inner discourse, not the other way around.

After you've practiced catching and eliminating these value judgments in a variety of situations, it starts to become second nature. You basically retrain your mind and create new mental habits for yourself. When you reach that point, your brain doesn't make the value judgment in the first place, and you are able to function without piling negative discourse on yourself. Of course it takes a lot of effort and time to do this, but you can start with small steps. The payoff is worth it, so keep trying! If you don't get it at first, don't be hard on yourself—just keep working at it.

PHYSICAL DEFINITION

Here's another valuable Stoic strategy for removing false judgments and seeing things clearly: physical definition.[4] It's simple but surprisingly effective. Most of the time as we react to the world, we perceive objects and events in their entirety. We see a car as a car, a child as a child, and a temper tantrum as a whole big tantrum. Our brains like to work efficiently, so they interpret objects in the biggest possible unit that makes sense. But there's another way of looking at things. You can break down an object into its component parts so that instead of seeing a whole car, you see wheels, doors, windows, headlights, and all its other parts. Or you could look at it as just certain types of materials: metal, rubber, glass, and so on.

What's the point of this thought experiment? It's another tool to help you step outside your everyday experience and get rid of your subjective value judgments. For example, Marcus Aurelius was the most powerful man on Earth during his life, and he easily could have let that fact go to his head. But as a Stoic philosopher, he knew there was nothing inherently wonderful about being emperor. He was a man just like any other, and he should be judged by his virtue, not by his royal robes. So he constantly reminded himself to see things objectively. He told himself that purple robes are just woven wool dyed with shellfish juice (which is how purple dye used to be made).[5] Expensive wine is really just fermented grape juice. All the prestige and status attached to such things is just opinion. It has nothing to do with your worth as a person.

We can take a similar approach in dealing with parenting challenges. Of course we are working in the opposite direction: Instead of keeping ourselves from being arrogant, we are keeping ourselves calm. But it works the same way. By breaking objects and situations into their components, we can recognize that they are not as good or as bad as we thought.

Let's go back to the temper tantrum. You could see it as a noisy, embarrassing situation, or you could see it as just a child crying and screaming when she doesn't get her way. The first definition brings in value judgments, which you know are just opinions. The second definition is much more factual and therefore closer to reality. If you see the tantrum from the second point of view, you are more accurate—and probably more tranquil.

You can break down pretty much any challenge in the same way. Is your child refusing to clean his room? Think about the parts of the situation: a frustrated parent; a dirty room; a boy who thinks other things in his life are more important than having a clean room or following his parents' directions. Remove your value judgment that this is a terrible situation, and focus on the components you can control. Did your daughter have a bad day at school? It's not the end of the world. Break down the problem into smaller parts, and help your daughter walk through what happened and what she can do better next time. Instead of looking at it as one huge, unsolvable problem, look at it as a series of small, solvable problems.

Just remember, there is always more than one way to look at a situation. If you feel yourself getting frustrated or angry, try to find a new perspective. From one perspective, the situation might seem like a total disaster; but from a different point of view, it's completely manageable. Try to see it through new eyes, either by removing your value judgment or by stepping back and breaking the problem down objectively. Yes, this is difficult to do in the heat of the moment, when you are upset and it seems like everything is falling apart. But just like we said before, it takes effort and practice to get good at it. Start applying this approach one challenge at a time, and you will start to change your way of seeing the world.

THE INNER CITADEL

Once you understand that the secret to tranquility is good judgment, life starts to look very different. You start to realize that a lot of your guilt, frustration, and stress is self-inflicted. It is also avoidable. Instead of stressing out about what other people think of your parenting skills, or whether you are doing things "right," you start to focus more on what is in your own control. You have a clear parenting philosophy to guide your actions, and you know how to use your inner discourse to make rational decisions based on that philosophy. You can feel more confident that you are doing the right thing.

Marcus Aurelius compares this sure, clear judgment to an inner refuge, a place that withstands all attacks from the outside world. He says, "Remember that your ruling faculty becomes invincible when it withdraws into itself and rests content with itself. . . . By virtue of this, an intelligence free from passions is a mighty citadel; for man has no stronghold more secure to which he can retreat."[6] In ancient times, a citadel was the strongest part of a castle or fortress, the last safe haven that remained standing during an attack. So it's very interesting that Marcus compares the innermost self to the innermost stronghold of a castle. This is where your deepest thoughts and feelings reside. The only way that external opinions can get into your inner citadel—your innermost self—is if you let them in. And it is completely up to you which external opinions you let into your mind.

Personally, I find it very helpful to think about my innermost self as a tower of strength. Whenever things get difficult, and when I feel like things are crashing down around my ears, I remember that I have an inner citadel that nothing can get past. My love for my children is always there with me, but many times the external situations I have to deal with stay outside this innermost refuge. My kids' misbehavior is just a situation that I have to deal with, not a reflection of my personal identity or my parenting skills.

What really struck me as a newly Stoic parent was how much more mental energy I could devote to the truly important tasks of parenting. When I was no longer moping or feeling guilty, I could enjoy my time with my children so much more. It didn't happen overnight, but once I had really worked to change my mental habits, I was able to catch and correct my self-defeating value judgments.

As you start rethinking your own judgments, keep in mind that you don't want to use Stoicism as an excuse to shut people out or ignore your responsibilities. It's not about running away from problems or emotions but about dealing with them more effectively. Remember to use this technique along with the parenting philosophy we outlined in chapter 1 and the dichotomy of control we talked about in chapter 2. In chapter 4 we will continue to apply Stoic techniques to interact success-fully and wisely with other people.

CHAPTER TAKEAWAYS

- We make unconscious value judgments about the world. This is necessary for things that are truly good or bad, but it can be harmful when applied to indifferent things.
- If you judge an indifferent situation to be good or bad, you are making an error of judgment. Things that do not affect your virtue are not inherently good or bad—they are just preferred or dispreferred indifferents.
- Many Stoics believe that most impressions consist of three parts: perception, interpretation, and value judgment. Value judgments are really just your opinion of how the event relates to your own ego. In order to see things as they really are, you should remove the value judgment and replace it with a decision and reaction. This helps eliminate your sense of injury from a situation and allows you to respond much more effectively.
- If you try to always be patient, despite feeling angry and upset, you will eventually run out of patience. Instead, remove your impression that something bad is happening to you. You will never run out of patience because you won't be upset in the first place.
- Another way to see things clearly is by physical definition. You break down an object or event into its parts or materials. This way, the problem no longer seems big and unmanageable because it's just a series of smaller components.
- Good judgment is your inner citadel. External things stay outside, and only your best thoughts are allowed in.

MAKE IT YOUR OWN

- Think about a scenario that often makes you mad or frustrated. Write down some of the value judgments you tend to make during this scenario. Are these judgments accurate? Are they true or false? Are they fact or opinion?
- Write down each value judgment on a separate piece of paper. Crumple them up one by one and throw them away![7] Consider this a symbolic gesture so that you can visualize doing the same thing the next time you catch yourself making negative value judgments.

- Make a list of five more situations that bring out the worst in you. Walk through the situations in your head and try to remember what you normally tell yourself while they're happening. Can you remember? If not, try to notice your inner discourse the next time you find yourself in that situation. Separate the facts from the opinions and see if you can eliminate negative opinions.
- Go back to the first frustrating scenario you imagined. Now try physical definition. Break down the situation into its components or materials. Try to think about it objectively. If you look at the situation as just a series of parts, does your ego really need to be involved?

4

ENGAGING WITH OTHER PEOPLE

Up to now we've talked mainly about how tranquility parenting depends on changing your internal discourse and developing a new way of seeing the world. But tranquility parenting, and Stoicism, is not merely about finding peace of mind. One very important component of Stoic philosophy is engaging with other people. This means fulfilling your social roles (as a parent, partner, neighbor, friend, etc.) and actively working to improve the world around you. The ancient Stoics were very involved in social and political life as governors, political advisors, diplomats, businessmen, teachers, mentors, and even, in the case of Marcus Aurelius, the Roman emperor. Stoicism has always been a practical philosophy designed to be used in all aspects of life, including social interactions.

In fact, Stoicism absolutely insists that we take action to help other people—no couch potatoes allowed. It all goes back to the idea that we should live "in accordance with nature." Humans are rational animals of course, but we are also social creatures. By our very nature we are made to live and work together. Because this is an important aspect of being human, we must do our best to pursue social obligations with wisdom, understanding, and enthusiasm.

Our primary concern in this book is your relationship with your child. But to have maximum clarity about this relationship, we need to back up for a moment and look at the general Stoic approach to ethics. How should we get along with other people? How can we maintain our tranquility when other people are so . . . well, you know how people are.

By answering this question, we can develop a strategy that will help us be kind and wise with our children. And by acting ethically toward others, we can model for our children how to deal effectively with challenging people and situations. When our children see us behaving with dignity and justice, they will start to learn how to do it for themselves.

We will start the chapter by looking at the general Stoic stance on ethics, or how we should behave toward others. As we do this, I will be discussing examples of how to apply these ideas to interacting with your child. At the end of the chapter, I will talk about how these same principles can apply to your relationships with other people, particularly those who might criticize your parenting.

There is one main theme that connects all these ideas on dealing with other people: No one makes mistakes on purpose. Let's take a look at what that means; then we'll see how it can help you engage with your child and other people.

NO ONE MAKES MISTAKES ON PURPOSE

Getting along with other people is one of the most difficult (but necessary) parts of life. The ancient Stoics were well aware of this. Consider for a moment what the three most famous Roman Stoics—Seneca, Epictetus, and Marcus Aurelius—had to go through. Seneca was political advisor to the evil emperor Nero, who killed many people to stay in power. Seneca's job was to try to convince Nero to do as little damage to the world as possible. Eventually Nero turned on him too and ordered Seneca to kill himself. Meanwhile, Epictetus was born a slave and may have had to endure a master who punished him by breaking one of his legs. He was later freed from slavery but remained lame his whole life. Marcus Aurelius saw several of his children die and had to deal with constant war and rebellion against the empire. Despite all their misfortunes and difficulties, these three Stoics were committed to the ideal of treating other people with fairness and benevolence. In other words, they were guided by a strong sense of justice.

Fortunately, most of us today do not have to deal with perpetual loss, enslavement, and maniacal dictators. Compared to such tragedies, dealing with a child's temper tantrum is literally child's play. However, we can adopt the same Stoic approach to life, knowing that this approach contains more than enough wisdom to guide us through our difficulties as modern parents.

What was it that allowed Seneca, Epictetus, and Marcus Aurelius to maintain their tranquility in dealing with other people? They understood that no one wants to act badly, but people often do act badly because they don't know any better.[1] (This idea was passed down to Stoicism from Socrates, another ancient philosopher who knew a thing or two about dealing with unpleasant people.) Most of the people we have to deal with simply do not know how to think clearly, and they do not know what virtue and true happiness are. No one wants to do things the wrong way, but some people have a misguided view of what "wrong" and "right" are. So, we should pity them rather than be angry at them.

Realizing that people usually do not want to act badly should make us more understanding toward them. This is especially true of children, who are mostly ignorant about the right way to do things. They simply haven't learned the best way to behave. Even if you've told them a million times not to use the couch as a trampoline, they don't understand that it really is in their best interest to follow the rules. To them, the immediate fun of bouncing all over the sofa outweighs your instructions and the vague potential of getting hurt. They are not trying to make your life terrible; it's just that they have mistakenly judged the best thing to do in that situation. Our job as parents is to correct their judgment, as far as possible for their age and developmental level.

Even older children do not have a fully developed understanding of what is in their best interest, which can lead them to make questionable decisions. A teenager might feel it's in his interest to play video games instead of doing homework, or to talk back to his parents when he's angry. But even though older children are really good at making you mad, it's still the same concept: They are acting in the way that seems right to them, which means they don't know any better. It's part of your role as a parent to enlighten them.

If you keep this in mind as you interact with your child, you will find it much easier to stay calm and patient. Your child's goal is not to do the wrong thing. Even though he probably can't articulate it, there is some cause for his behavior. He might be trying to get attention, express his frustration, or assert his independence—or maybe he's just tired and hungry. Maybe you'll never know the reason. But the underlying cause is the same: He hasn't learned the right way to behave. That means he needs more guidance from you.

That doesn't mean you should just let him jump on the sofa or play video games whenever he wants. But it does help you to be kind and understanding while you correct him. You don't have to see every little misbehavior as a conflict of wills. If you take it as a personal insult that he is not following your instructions, you will get angry, and you will discipline out of anger. If you don't take his misbehavior as a personal insult, you can discipline out of a desire to teach. Just remember that your child doesn't yet understand what is best for him in the long run (i.e., doing what you ask him to). He lacks experience and understanding, and therefore he makes bad decisions about what is in his best interest.

CONFLICT OF INTEREST

So how do you deal with misbehavior? Start with the idea that your child does not know what is in her best interest. Epictetus says that if you can convince someone that acting rightly is in his or her best interest, that person will change his or her behavior. He uses the example of a thief: "Since someone who commits an error doesn't want to do that, but to act rightly, it is clear that he isn't doing what he wants. For what does a thief want to achieve? Something that is to his benefit. If theft, then, is contrary to his benefit, he isn't doing what he wants."[2] In other words, thieves steal because they think it is better for them to steal than to not steal. But if you can convince the thief that it's better for him to not steal, he will end his thieving ways.

Just substitute "child" for "thief" in this passage and you have a perfect explanation for why kids misbehave. What does a child want to achieve? His own benefit. If he realizes that a behavior is bad for him, he will change it. This is the key to changing a child's behavior: convincing the child that it better to do as the parent asks. As Epictetus observes, "Someone who is skilled in reasoning, and is able both to encourage and to refute, will thus be able to show each person the contradiction that is causing him to go astray. . . . For if anyone can make that clear to him, he'll renounce his error of his own accord, but if you fail to show him, don't be surprised if he persists in it, being under the impression that he is acting rightly."[3]

So, all you have to do is convince your child that misbehavior is not in her best interest. Piece of cake, right? (Yes, I'm kidding.) But this does give us a place to start dealing with problematic behavior. You just have to change the calculation of benefit for your child until she realizes that she really is better off following your directions. This is where wisdom and patience come in. Wisdom, because you must think about your child's age, life experiences, temperament, and all the other things that motivate behavior. Patience, because you might have to try a few different techniques to find the ones that work best. It might be explanation, encouragement, reminders, one type of reward, or a different type of reward. It might be a combination of things. You just have to show your child that listening to you is more to her benefit than all the fun she could have by jumping on the couch.

For children old enough to understand, you might be able to deploy logic to explain why following directions is in their best interest. When five-year-old Clementine balked at brushing her teeth, logic was very effective at making her change her mind. "Clementine, do you want your teeth to rot out?" my husband asked her. "Do you want the dentist to drill a hole into your teeth?" She quickly ran into the bathroom to brush her teeth. I often point out to my kids—as have many parents throughout history: "Do you think I made up this rule just for fun? Do you think I ask you buckle up just because I like to hear seatbelts click? Or is it because I want to keep you safe if something crashes into our car?" This way even James, at three and a half, understands that it's in his best interest to keep his seatbelt on.

On the other hand, sometimes explaining things just doesn't work. In that case, you must change the calculation of benefit in other ways. If James won't stay buckled up because he knows it's the right thing to do, then maybe he will stay buckled if he gets chewing gum . . . or gets to ride with the window down . . . or gets to listen to his favorite song on the way. Just try to approach this trial-and-error process as a learning experience, not as a recipe for frustration.

In my experience, the more children are exposed to logical reasoning, the more they are able to understand it. Obviously, there are developmental stages that cannot be ignored. But why not start talking to your kids early about moral reasoning? It does take some of your time and energy, but it also helps them understand that you don't make decisions arbitrarily. They may not completely understand your reasoning, but at least they will know that you refer to an ethical code to guide your actions. And with enough practice and encouragement, they might just learn to use the same reasoning and ethical code to guide their own actions.

Just to clarify, you can't expect young children, or even older children, to be logical in the same way that adults are logical. (Many adults aren't all that logical, either.) But you can at least start the process. You can show them that you understand they might have a reason for wanting to take a piece of candy without asking but that you also have reasons for expecting them to mind. Young children often can't articulate their emotions or thought processes. But the earlier you start talking about it, the sooner they will have the words and concepts to express themselves. It will take patience, but building a moral vocabulary will pay off for all of you in the long run.

EXPECT TO DEAL WITH PROBLEMS

Marcus Aurelius had to deal with a lot of unpleasant people. Even though he was probably the most powerful man on Earth, he did not like living among the flatterers, backstabbers, and gossips at court (not to mention the rebels trying to break away from the empire). But because he still felt an enormous responsibility to behave ethically toward his subjects and try to be a wise ruler, he adopted some interesting coping techniques for dealing with other people. As parents who may be dealing with our own little rebels at home, I think we can apply some of these same techniques.

For one thing, Marcus Aurelius suggests that we don't kid ourselves about the way other people are. We should prepare ourselves to deal with all the negative traits people might have: greed, betrayal, meanness, pettiness, everything. It's unrealistic to expect that other people will be nice to you all the time. Yes, we should do our best to work for a society in which people are always nice to one another. But until that day comes, it's foolish to go out into the world expecting all sunshine and rainbows. Therefore, he advises us, "Say to yourself at the start of the day, 'I shall meet with meddling, ungrateful, violent, treacherous, envious, and unsociable people. They are subject to all these defects because they have no knowledge of good and bad.'"[4]

In other words, from the time we get up in the morning, we should consciously prepare ourselves to deal with problems. This is not pessimistic; it's realistic. To be wise, you must face things as they really are. But what sets the Stoic viewpoint apart from others is the attitude underlying this sense of realism. We shouldn't be jaded cynics in our dealings with others. Remember, Stoics think people do bad things not because they are bad at heart but because they just don't know any better. They are simply misguided. It is our job to bear with them patiently and exhibit the Stoic virtues of gentleness, forgiveness, kindness, and benevolence.

Let's modify this idea a little for dealing with our kids. Realistically, you know your child is not perfect. You know this because (a) no one is perfect and (b) you have experience with your child. You probably know what his tendencies are and what might cause potential conflicts. Rather than being caught off guard, it's better to be prepared and have an action plan in mind.

It's a good idea to begin each day by mentally preparing ourselves to deal with problems. This is one type of Stoic "premeditation of adversity." We know that unpleasant behaviors are bound to happen sometimes. But if we take time to think about potential problems, we can face them much more easily. For instance, if you know your child has a hard time getting up in the morning, you can take steps to make the process flow more smoothly. Prepare him the night before: Get his clothes and lunchbox ready, talk to him about the steps you will both go through to get ready for school. Set his alarm five minutes earlier if necessary. Make a checklist to keep him on track. Check in with him frequently to see if he's brushed his teeth or gotten his shoes on yet. Praise him for getting things done quickly.

The point is, if you give some thought to potential problem areas, you will be prepared to deal with them. You will always be better off if you anticipate problems and are ready for them. Sometimes, challenges might arise unexpectedly with things you didn't anticipate. That's OK— Stoics know to expect the unexpected. You can be mentally prepared for the unexpected simply by knowing that unpleasant things happen sometimes. Even if you didn't foresee a particular problem, you have a general expectation that your day will not be perfect. Expect to deal with challenges, and you will never be surprised when challenges arise.

INSTRUCT THEM OR PUT UP WITH THEM

If you are prepared to deal with the unpleasant side of things, you can be proactive in a difficult situation. One way to be proactive is to approach the situation as a teacher. Maybe this is an opportunity to teach the other person how to see things through the lens of virtue and tranquility. As Marcus says, "If he goes wrong, instruct him in a kindly manner, show him what he failed to see; but if you are unable to, blame only yourself, or not even yourself."[5]

This advice is particularly apt for us as parents. Unlike the Roman emperor, we don't have authority over the adults around us. But we do have authority over our children. When Marcus says, "Human beings have come into the world for the sake of one another; either instruct them, then, or put up with them,"[6] we can do that with our kids. We should correct their behavior and teach them how to be good people. But remember, we don't actually control our kids, so sometimes our teaching may not have the desired effect. There may be some things that we just have to put up with.

As teachers, we should strive to be kind and understanding. That does not mean you should never be stern or firm with your child. On the contrary, sometimes you do need to be stern to help your child understand the consequences of her behavior. But you can be firm without being harsh or angry. You can instruct without yelling. You can discipline while maintaining your tranquility. And you can do it "in no sarcastic or reproachful spirit, but affectionately, and with a heart free from rancor."[7]

This is the heart of the matter (literally and figuratively). In tranquility parenting, we discipline out of affection, not frustration. Misbehavior is an indication that your child does not understand the right way to act. She needs extra guidance, which you might give in the form of explanation, correction, or other discipline. Misbehavior is not a cause for anger, irritation, despair, guilt, blame, or any other negative feelings. Nobody likes dealing with misbehavior, but we know it's going to happen sometimes. We can plan for it, try to minimize it, and look for the most effective forms of correction. What we should *not* do is see it as a negative reflection of our child's personality (she'll grow up to be a thief!) or our own identity (I'm a horrible parent!).

Instead we should remember that everyone in the situation is acting in the way that makes sense to him or her. We are all doing our best here. You are doing your best as the parent, and your child is doing what seems best to her from her childish perspective. Try to be patient with yourself and with her.

You might wonder how you could discipline your child effectively if you don't yell and look angry. Won't your child mind better if she thinks you're angry? It's true that anger is sometimes effective at motivating people. But think of it this way: If your child is only motivated by your anger, then you will have to get angry (or threaten to get angry) every time you want her to do something. Isn't it more effective in the long run to find a different way of motivating her? Another thought: Even if your daughter is motivated by your anger, you have to give up your own tranquility (and virtue) in order to motivate her. Is that a good exchange? I don't think so. If you're serious about achieving tranquility and virtue—for yourself and your child—it makes a lot more sense to adopt Marcus's approach.

A final reason to stay calm while you correct your child is that he will learn the best way to get along with other people. If you take out your frustration by yelling at him, he will learn to deal with his own frustrations that way. If you solve problems by getting angry and fighting with people, he will probably adopt the same behaviors. But if you consistently demonstrate that you can solve problems with patience and affection, you will plant the seed for him to do the same. Not that he will automatically learn to be patient—because we all know patience is very hard to acquire—but at least he will have a good role model to learn from.

DEALING WITH OTHER PEOPLE'S OPINIONS

As parents, it might seem straightforward enough for us to treat our children with kindness, patience, and understanding. After all, we love our children and are committed to their well-being. But our commitment to ethical behavior should go beyond just treating our children well. If we wish to find lasting tranquility, we should behave well toward everyone else too. Why? Because, as Marcus says, "We have come into being to work together, like feet, hands, eyelids, or the two rows of teeth in our upper and lower jaws. To work against one another is therefore contrary to nature."[8]

We do not live in isolation, but in families and communities. Part of our role as parents is to demonstrate for our children how to get along with others. Remember that your child learns how to live her life by watching you live yours. If you respond with anger and frustration to life's challenges, that's what she will do too. But if you respond with grace and good humor, you are showing your child how to do the same.

Even though this book is primarily focused on you and your child, I'd like to discuss a situation that most parents must deal with at some point: other people's negative opinions about your parenting style. As every parent knows, there are huge social pressures for us to raise our kids in a certain way. These pressures come from every direction: media, parenting books, friends, colleagues, family members, random people on the Internet, people standing next to us in the checkout line. It seems like everyone wants to tell us what to do, even when we least expect it.

For example, one Saturday my husband took our car to the hardware store to get some lumber. He moved the child car seat to the front so that he could fit the fence posts in the back. (The kids weren't with him, so it wasn't a big deal.) But when he got back to the car with his purchase, someone had left a note on the windshield scolding him for putting a child in the front seat. "Small children should never be in the front seat!" the note said, with underlines and exclamation points. Apparently, we are never far from other people's judgments and assumptions, even when we go to the store alone.

Clearly, there is no single right way to be a parent or raise your kids. Most children turn out OK, regardless of their upbringing, and many even turn out great. (And no one so far has turned out to be perfect.) But as we saw in chapter 2, even if there *were* one right way to do things, you *still* couldn't guarantee how your child would turn out. There are so many other factors involved—external circumstances, accidents, genes, etc.—most of which you do not control.

Just as you do not have complete control over your children, you also do not have control over other people. One thing Stoicism helped me realize is that what other people do or say has everything to do with them and very little to do with me. Let's say there actually were a perfect person on Earth. What do you think people would say about her? Some would admire, respect, and try to emulate her, but others would find something to criticize about her out of envy, malice, boredom, or ignorance. They might even criticize her for being too perfect. But the reasons those people have for criticism do not reflect the qualities of the person being criticized (who is, in our hypothetical example, perfect). They reflect the shortcomings of the person doing the criticizing.

Most people don't see themselves as being malicious or wrong when they criticize others; they actually think they are right. They may believe they are helping others through their criticism or believe they're setting the world right. Remember, Epictetus says that people don't do "bad" things because they want to be bad but because they think what they are doing is the right thing to do. They don't do "annoying" things because they want to be annoying (unless they are three years old). For whatever reasons, doing those things makes sense to them.

From a Stoic perspective, criticizers are simply deprived of the truth. You might call them misguided in three ways: (1) They think others are wrong and they are right; (2) they think they have the right to criticize something they perceive to be wrong; and (3) they think their criticism is important and necessary. Obviously, there are certain times when criticism *is* justified and when it *is* the right thing to do. But it requires wisdom to know when criticism is appropriate and when it is not. Many people lack the necessary wisdom to make a good decision about this. Therefore, the first step in dealing with other people's negative opinions is to remember that the criticizer is misguided.

Let's take an example. Someone (it could be anyone—a friend, family member, teacher, neighbor) insinuates that you don't discipline your kids the "right" way. What is an appropriately Stoic reaction to criticism of your parenting style? First of all, this takes us back to classic Stoic teachings: Everything depends on how you interpret it. Even if someone means to insult or criticize you, you have a choice about how to interpret those remarks. Just because someone says something critical does not mean you have to be upset or offended.

If we have a choice about how to receive criticism, how do we do it? Remember that criticism mainly reflects the qualities of the criticizer.

When someone criticizes us, it's a good idea to reflect on her character and intentions, as well as our relationship with her. Are you dealing with someone who cares about your child? If you think she truly wants what is best for you, you at least owe it to her to consider her opinion. You might decide, after reflection, that even though she really wants the best for you, she is misguided in her understanding of what is best. Even if you don't take her advice, you will at least have considered your options with an open mind.

On the other hand, if you determine that the criticizer is not close to you and/or does not have your best interests at heart, you can ignore or deflect the criticism. That would include the opinions of celebrities on TV, friends of friends, people standing in the checkout line at the store, and parents you meet at other kids' birthday parties. Do you have any good reason to care about what they think? No. Maybe everyone in the world has an opinion on how you should raise your child, but many of them are not close to you or are not qualified to give their opinion. You can choose not to listen.

It also helps to learn to expect some criticism from others. Just as you can expect misbehavior from your child, you can also expect unhelpful behavior from other people in the world. And just as you can premeditate solutions to your child's problems, you can reflect in advance on how to deal with criticism. After all, why should we expect to have a life free of problems or criticism? That is never going to happen. Instead of expecting everyone else in the world to agree with me, I should focus on my own side of the interaction. I can't control what other people think, say, or do. But I can make my own mind harmonious by adjusting it to the reality of the situation.

I admit, it has been much harder for me to deal with criticism as a parent than it was in my childless days. Before I had kids, it was not too difficult to shrug off criticism. I could tell myself that it didn't matter what other people thought of me. But when people start suggesting that you are ruining your kids, it can really get to you. I often found myself brooding over someone's remarks, even though I knew in my heart that person was wrong. It was only after I learned about Stoicism that I had the proper tools to cope with other people's opinions.

The other side of the coin is that we should make sure we are not criticizers ourselves. It's very easy to judge others—and very hard to understand them. You might look at other parents on the playground and think they are doing things wrong, that your own methods are better than theirs. Or you might have the opposite opinion and think other people are doing things better than you. Both angles are just problems of judgment. Remember that our tranquility parenting philosophy calls for us to think clearly and use good judgment.

In fact, Stoicism is quite clear that you should refrain from judging other people about indifferent things. (However, if you see someone doing something unethical or malicious, you should not only judge but also take action.) Just because another parent handles things differently than you does not make her wrong and you right. There might be many factors behind the scenes that you do not know about. As Marcus says, "You cannot even be certain that what they are doing is wrong; for many actions are undertaken for some ulterior purpose and, as a general rule, you must find out a great deal before you can deliver a properly founded judgment on the actions of others."[9] Try to be understanding rather than judgmental. We all act in the way that makes sense to us.

In the next chapter we will talk more about how to use these ethical principles to engage with your child. As we do, keep in mind the key concept from this chapter: Your child acts in the way that seems best to him, given his childish experience and perspective on the world. Our goal in chapter 5 will be teaching our kids how to make good decisions about what is best so that we can help them to live a flourishing and happy life.

CHAPTER TAKEAWAYS

- Stoicism insists that people are made to live and work together, so getting along well with others is part of being wise. By modeling good social behavior, we can help teach our children to act wisely toward others.
- People act badly only because they don't know any better. We should pity them rather than get angry at them.
- Your child's goal is not to do the wrong thing. He just hasn't learned the right way to behave. That means he needs more guidance from you.
- You don't have to see every little misbehavior as a conflict of wills. If you take it as a personal insult that your child is not following your

instructions, you will get angry, and you will discipline out of anger. If you don't take it as a personal insult, you can discipline out of a desire to teach.

- Children act in their own interest. To correct misbehavior, help your child understand that misbehaving is not in her interest.
- Expose your child to moral reasoning from an early age. Talk about your own decision-making process. This helps her understand that you don't make decisions arbitrarily and that you refer to an ethical code to guide your actions. The earlier you start building a moral vocabulary, the sooner she will have the words and concepts she needs to talk about her own actions.
- Expect to deal with problems. Take time each day to think about potential challenges with your child and how you can deal with them.
- Approach problems as a teacher. First instruct your kids; if that doesn't work, then accept them as they are. There may be some lessons they are not ready to learn. But whatever you do, do it with kindness and understanding.
- Be ethical with everyone you know, not just your children. This will help you achieve virtue and tranquility. It will also teach your children the right way to deal with other people.
- Here's a summary of the steps we discussed for handling criticism from other adults:

  1. Remember that the criticizer is misguided. He probably thinks he is doing the right thing.
  2. Choose not to be offended. Remember, only your own attitude and opinions are completely up to you. You can't control what other people think.
  3. Think about the source of the criticism: Is it someone close to your child who truly has his best interests at heart? If so, carefully consider whether you should accept the advice. If not, then feel free to ignore or reject the criticism.
  4. Think of criticism as a dispreferred indifferent, like getting sick. Nobody wants it to happen, but it still happens sometimes. It doesn't mean you're a bad person—it's just something that happens to you.

5. Expect to be criticized at some point. Spend time thinking about how you should respond to criticism when you encounter it. If you're prepared, you can handle it gracefully.
6. Don't be a criticizer yourself. Try not to judge other parents; you never know what is going on behind the scenes. They are doing what makes sense to them.

MAKE IT YOUR OWN

- Do you agree with the idea that people do not intentionally act badly but simply do not know the appropriate way to behave? Can you think of specific situations when this applies to your child?
- Brainstorm strategies you could use to convince your child that following your directions is in his own interest. The next time he misbehaves, try one of these strategies. If it doesn't work the first time, try again, or think about a different strategy to use on the next occasion.
- Try the premeditation of adversity. Make a list of all the potential problems you could face tomorrow with your child. Then identify an appropriate response for each problem. The next time a problem arises, you will already have a solution for dealing with it.
- Think back to a situation when you had to deal with someone's criticism. How did you respond? Do you think a Stoic perspective would have helped you respond better? Now think about how you would respond following the steps from this chapter. Try to go through the entire situation in your head, with you staying calm and dealing wisely with the criticism.
- Brainstorm different situations in which someone is likely to criticize your parenting abilities or methods. Think calmly about the criticizer's motivations. Try to feel empathy for that person. Create a real response that involves kindness and understanding. I know it's hard to imagine yourself being kind when you receive criticism, but try to imagine yourself saying those words to the person. Maybe eventually you will really be able to say them!

5

TEACHING YOUR CHILD VIRTUE

You might find it strange that in a book about parenting, we haven't talked much about what you should actually do with your child. We've discussed your parenting philosophy and how you can change your perspective to stay calm, consistent, confident, and kind. If you've already started putting these techniques into practice, I hope you've found that these on their own make a wonderful difference in your time with your child.

But another important dimension of parenting is how you should engage with your child. Raising children is not just about being a good parent; it's also about teaching your child to become a good person. Just as we teach our kids how to talk, ride a bicycle, and drive a car, we teach them how to approach life and respond to difficulties. And while we can't *control* what they do and who they become, we can help them find their own path to flourishing. So part of our task in tranquility parenting is figuring out how to impart wisdom and good judgment to our children.

For me, one of the greatest benefits of Stoic parenting is having a built-in set of guidelines for teaching my children. I've always wanted the best for my kids, but before I encountered Stoicism, I had no clear sense of what "wanting the best" actually meant. Does it mean buying the candy bar or not buying the candy bar? Stoicism helps us answer this question by defining what "the best" is: *eudaimonia*—the lasting, fulfilling, rich happiness that results from a life well lived. *Eudaimonia* is "a condition in which a person of excellent character is living optimally well, flourishing, doing admirably, and steadily enjoying the best mindset that is available to human beings."[1] Could it get any better than that? Don't we all want that for our children?

If you agree that *eudaimonia* is a good goal, then you understand that it is vital to teach virtue. *Eudaimonia* results from applying wisdom and virtue to everyday living. So your path becomes clear. All the other good things you might want for your child—academic success, rewarding relationships, eventual career and financial success—are secondary to helping him find *eudaimonia*. These other things can go alongside virtue and complement it, but they should not be mistaken as the path to happiness. We have all heard countless examples of externally successful people who were miserable, or of people who did not achieve worldly success but were honorable and content. The Stoics say that everyone wants to be happy, but most people do not know the right way to achieve happiness.

So what is the right way? I think we can adapt Stoic philosophy to start teaching virtue in developmentally appropriate ways even from a young age. Below, we will see exactly what that means, and then we will look at specific, practical ways you can start teaching virtue. Does that sound good? Let's get started.

CAN YOU TEACH VIRTUE?

As we've said from the very beginning, tranquility doesn't come from nowhere. That's true for your child's life as well as your own. The good news is, the path to tranquility and happiness is basically the same for everyone: Think clearly, act wisely, and deal with indifferents as best you can. No matter what your age, you can work toward excellence in your own (age-appropriate) way.

One ancient Stoic teacher, Gaius Musonius Rufus, describes how we can begin teaching even the youngest children to be virtuous: "We must start by teaching infants that this thing is good and that thing is bad, that this thing is helpful and that thing is harmful, and that this thing must be done and that thing must not be done."[2] This advice may sound a bit obvious, but I think it's a great starting point for us to teach virtue. We don't have to teach kids abstract principles or theory. We just start teaching them good judgment.

Once children understand what is good and bad, Musonius says, their understanding will lead them to be self-controlled, disciplined, and courageous. The correctly educated person will know how to work hard and deal with setbacks. And, as Musonius points out, "Surely to shun excess, to honor equality, to want to do good, and for a person, being human, to not want to harm human beings—this is the most honorable lesson and it makes just people out of those who learn it."[3]

The challenge of course is translating all this to our real life as parents in the twenty-first century. There are different ways you could teach virtue, but in my experience the crucial ingredient is the simplest: Talk about virtue with your child. All the time. Everywhere. Talk about why you make the decisions you do: "I feel frustrated right now, but I'm staying calm so that I can solve the problem." Talk about your expectations for her behavior: "I expect you to be kind to your little brother—snatching is not allowed in our house." Talk about the ethical consequences of her actions: "I'm so proud of you for sharing!" or "Do you feel proud of yourself for helping your brother?" Some things that seem obvious to us as adults are really not obvious to children. Explain your moral reasoning whenever possible so that your child understands that she needs to go through the same thought process for her own actions.

Talking about virtue with your child has many benefits. The most immediate consequence is that your child will hopefully modify his current behavior. (Remember, in chapter 4 we said that if you can convince your child that being good is in his best interest, he will be good.) If he sees that snatching makes his friend sad, he will start to understand why he shouldn't snatch. If you cultivate his sense of empathy from a young age, he will be more likely to behave for the right reasons rather than simply out of fear of punishment.

But the long-term benefits of talking about virtue are even more important. First, your child will learn to think and talk about his own behavior. Children are not born with the words and concepts to discuss ethics. We have to teach them. If you give your child the vocabulary to talk about his impulses and actions, he will be in a much better position to use that vocabulary with you, with other adults, and with himself. And not only will he have the words he needs, but he can learn the habit of stopping to think about his actions and their consequences.

The second important long-term benefit is that your child will learn that her actions should proceed from her ethics. This is especially important for older children and teens. By talking about your moral reasoning for your own actions, you demonstrate that you don't act at random. Your actions are guided by certain beliefs. And when you tell her that her actions should also comply with a set of core beliefs, you help her (slowly) develop a similar reference point for herself. She shouldn't do things simply because she wants to; she should do things because they're the right thing to do.

It may sound odd to talk to a child about ethical decision making. But you can actually find ways to incorporate it very naturally into everyday life. For instance, when Clementine complained about not wanting to make her bed in the morning, I reminded her that I also have to do things I don't want to do. "Do you think I should skip making dinner tonight, since I don't like to cook? Or should I not buy you any clothes because I don't like shopping? Making the bed is just part of life." She quickly understood and started making her bed. And, I'm happy to report, she still gets up every morning and makes her bed before leaving her room.

Having this external reference point for our ethics has transformed my relationship with my children. Before Stoicism, I made decisions based on intuition, circumstances, experience, and spur-of-the-moment beliefs. My children did the same. If I made a decision they didn't like, I didn't have anything to back it up besides my status as the parent. It became a contest of wills—my will versus their wills. In other words, a constant power struggle.

Once I started using Stoic virtue as a guide for my actions and my kids' actions, I noticed a change in everyone's attitude. My children seem to respond much better to correction when I refer to universal principles rather than mere parental authority. If I appeal to their innate sense of social concern, and teach them to reason for themselves, they are more likely to act wisely in the long term. We do what is right because it is the right thing to do, not just because it's what Mom said to do. I don't ask them to be kind just because I want them to be kind; I ask them to be kind because it's the right thing to do. How do we know it's the right thing to do? Because being kind is part of being a good person.

At the moment, my children are still too young to understand anything as abstract as "virtue" and "flourishing." It would be silly to talk about such abstractions with a three- or five-year-old. But the principles behind our actions are there so that as they grow up, I can start talking about virtue and *eudaimonia* with them. Since we are establishing our ethical reference points at a young age, we can start building on a firm foundation. They already have the words, concepts, and habits for virtuous behavior.

THE PATH TO FLOURISHING

Enough with the theory, you might be thinking. *How do I actually do this with my child?* The easiest way is to start with the three principles of our tranquility parenting philosophy and package them in a way our children can understand. Remember, we derived this parenting philosophy from the basic principles of Stoicism. By adapting these beliefs for our children, we are able to teach them the same core beliefs we use to guide our own behavior. It's the ultimate technique for clarity and consistency.

Let's quickly review the core beliefs from our tranquility parenting philosophy:

1. **Thinking clearly.** We should use our reason to have consistent, coherent parenting principles that direct our behavior. We should learn to bypass negative emotions so that we can deal with challenges more effectively.
2. **Acting wisely.** We should apply the virtues in all our actions. When we interact with our child, we demonstrate the beliefs and behaviors we think are important.
3. **Dealing with indifferents.** There will always be some undesirable situations we have to confront as parents. The way we choose to deal with indifferent things is up to us.

When I sat down to think about how I could teach these core Stoic principles to my children, I came up with some very basic concepts that we use every day. Many of these are just common guidelines of behavior that parents and teachers have always taught children. In a way, that's kind of the point. There's nothing new about teaching kids to use good judgment. But what has been very helpful for me is understanding the connection between ethical teaching and theory. As you go through daily life with your child, you can consistently refer back to your own philosophy to help you make decisions and guide your child. Just as it is helpful to have core beliefs as a parent, it is helpful to have kid-friendly core beliefs ready to teach.

In the kid-friendly version, I've used the same headings we use in our parenting philosophy, but there is also a child-appropriate slogan you can teach your child. You'll notice that there is some overlap between the three principles, which is no coincidence. They reinforce one another!

Here's what our three Stoic principles look like when you teach them to your child:

1. **Thinking clearly > You control yourself, not other people.** Learn to think about your own thoughts and actions, and focus on your own behavior, not other people's behavior.
2. **Acting wisely > Treat other people the way you want them to treat you.** Learn to think about things from another person's perspective, help other people, and be a kind friend/sibling.
3. **Dealing with indifferents > Don't get upset, just deal with the problem.** Develop self-awareness and emotional control, be patient, and deal with frustration, fear, and discomfort.

One psychological technique the ancient Stoics perfected is creating short, easy-to-remember phrases you can keep in mind as you go about daily life. Stoicism is an applied philosophy, meaning it's meant to be used in everyday life. The ancients knew that people will always face difficult situations in real time, not sitting in an armchair reading a book. So they developed short slogans and maxims you can pull out whenever you need them.

I've tried to preserve these clear, memorable phrases in our tranquility parenting philosophy so that you can remember them even when you are exhausted and frazzled. It's the same with these kid-friendly maxims, which are simple enough to start teaching to a two-year-old. (Not that a two-year-old will "get" them for a while, but you can start teaching the concepts.)

The good thing about these principles is that they work for everyone, from birth through old age. So you can start teaching them at a young age and adapt them as your child grows up. Most of the examples I provide in this chapter relate to young children because, at the moment, my children are still young. But these principles are for everyone. If you have a tween or teen, you can take the same ideas and adapt them for your child's age and maturity level. Older children are much better with logic and reasoning, so it's more straightforward to explain ethical concepts to them—although that doesn't always mean they will comply! So even though the focus here is on young children, I will also mention some ways you can apply the same principles to all age groups.

Let's look in more detail at how you can integrate these central Stoic principles into your parenting. I'm going to discuss them in reverse order, because *thinking clearly* is actually the most advanced and difficult to teach. We will work our way up to that one. Remember that these are just a few examples; these same principles could be applied in many different real-life situations. The possibilities are truly endless!

DON'T GET UPSET, JUST DEAL WITH THE PROBLEM

As parents, we have a special opportunity to instruct our children as they learn about the world. One important lesson we can teach is how to stay calm in the face of frustration and difficulties. For example, when your child gets frustrated because he can't do something by himself, what do you tell him? This is a teachable moment for virtue. Rather than just telling him to try harder or stop crying, you can help change his value judgment about the situation. Remember how we practiced rethinking our own value judgments in chapter 3? We can help our children do the same thing.

The genius of Stoic psychology is treating the so-called illness (mistaken beliefs) rather than the symptoms (frustration, anger, fear) of negative emotions. If you just treat the symptoms by telling your child to stay calm, you don't actually change the root cause of the behavior. The root cause is a mistaken belief that "I can't get my shoes on, and it is bad." Eventually he will learn to get his shoes on, but he will then apply the same mistaken beliefs to other situations in life: "I can't get the video game I want, and it is bad." "I can't get the girlfriend I want, and it is bad." "I can't get the job I want, and it is bad." The pattern repeats itself and becomes an ingrained mental habit. This is how we find ourselves as adults holding mistaken judgments about the world.

When your child gets upset, you can go straight to the mistaken value judgment that is causing him to feel frustrated. "Is this something to get upset about?" I ask James when he can't get his shoes on. Usually the answer is no. I try to help him keep things in perspective, on his level: "Are you about to fall in a volcano? No. Are you about to get struck by lightning? No. Are you about to get eaten by a dinosaur?" No, he giggles, and starts to realize this is nothing to get upset about.

Even though young children don't understand abstract terms like reason and rationality, I talk with my kids about how their brain is their superpower that they can use to solve problems. This seems to get through to them. (Although sometimes Clementine insists that her *real* superpower is freezing people like the Disney princess Elsa, and James says he would rather fly.) When they are starting to get upset, I remind them that their smart brains can help them stay calm. They like using their superpower. I'm sure different families may develop different ways of talking about these principles, but I think the main point is to find metaphors and concrete references your kids can understand.

We constantly talk about solving problems, so they know it is something I value highly and we devote a lot of energy to. We solve problems ranging from running out of napkins at the dinner table to disagreeing about what book to read. We talk to one another about our disagreements—we use our words to solve problems so that we don't have to hit, push, or throw. I encourage them to use their eyes to see the problem, their brains to find a solution, and their hands to fix the problem. When someone has solved a problem, we congratulate and celebrate.

However, another way of dealing with problems is to just accept things the way they are. Sometimes you can't change the world to suit you, so you have to change yourself to adapt to the world. Learning that they can't have everything they want is another difficult but necessary lesson for kids. You can teach this lesson anywhere and everywhere. If you're in the store and your child wants another toy, you can remind her that she already has plenty of toys and doesn't need another one. If you're at the dinner table and she wants another scoop of ice cream, it's time to practice not getting what she wants. Just remember, there is a reason you are making her practice this: so that she can learn virtue and find the path to happiness and flourishing. She will never be happy in life if she thinks she will always get her own way. She will learn to be happy if she knows she *won't* always get her own way and learns how to deal with it.

For older kids (and adults) who are still dealing with issues like patience and problem solving, identifying and clarifying the problem are important first steps. Even older children are not always aware of their emotions, so it's helpful to make them aware of what's behind their frustration. Help them understand that there are solutions to frustration, and that they will become a smart, capable person by learning how to deal with problems. Try to be positive (Let's find a solution!) rather than negative (Why are you so short-tempered?). See it as an opportunity to teach skills and resourcefulness. Children can be very sensitive to hovering and criticism, so try to approach the situation with empathy. You can be calm, authoritative, and respectful of your child's feelings all at the same time.

TREAT OTHER PEOPLE THE WAY YOU WANT THEM TO TREAT YOU

As rational adults, we can think about how our actions will affect those around us on many different levels, ranging from immediate family members to local community members to someone on the other side of the world. But how do you begin to teach this to young children?

As clichéd as it is, one way is to start with the Golden Rule. The way I put it is "Treat other people the way you want them to treat you." We talk about this rule *a lot* at my house. Whenever Clementine and James do something unkind to each other, this rule comes out: "James, do you want Clementine to take your toy away? No. Then don't do it to her. Clementine, do you want James to yell at you? No. Then don't yell at him."

You could say that the whole purpose of ethics for young children is teaching them to get outside themselves and think about the consequences of their actions. Learning ethics is all about learning your place within the human community and therefore understanding how your behavior impacts other people. Most of the rules and principles I teach my kids relate to seeing the world from a universal perspective rather than from their own egocentric perspective. Here are some that I find myself using often:

- If you can't say something nice, don't say anything at all. (Yes, this is an old-fashioned saying, but it still works.)
- James, are you being kind right now? No. Then change your behavior.
- Clementine, do you like to listen to James whine? No. Then do you think we like to hear you whine?
- We are a family and we treat each other nicely. Even if you are frustrated with your brother, you still love him and you still have to be nice. You are never allowed to do mean things, even if you are mad. Find a better way to solve the problem.

Another good strategy is to praise your child when they work hard at an ethical action. When you see that your kids have done something kind, or refrained from doing something inappropriate, be sure to compliment them:

- I know you're really hungry, so I appreciate you waiting for everyone else to start eating.
- I'm so proud of you for sharing with your sister.
- Thank you for helping your brother get his toy. That was very sweet of you.

You can also help them feel proud of themselves when they do something good:

- Don't you feel proud of yourself for helping your brother?
- Doesn't it feel good to do something nice for him?
- You get good feelings when you do good things.

Which leads to another abstract virtue that can be difficult to teach: Material things are not as important as being a good person. When James wants to take the ball Freddy is playing with, I ask him, "Which is more important—having the ball or being a good brother?" If Clementine doesn't want to let James have a turn with a toy, I'll say, "Which is more important—having the toy all to yourself, or being a good sharer?" I let her make the decision. When we frame things that way, she usually admits that it's better to share and lets James have a turn. (James almost always returns the favor later.)

When it comes to encouraging your child to help around the house or participate in family activities, I think it's helpful to emphasize the communal nature of being a family. We all have certain roles to play in the family, and we all have certain responsibilities to each other. Parents take care of their kids, and kids have to follow their parents' directions. I've found it very helpful to point out to my children that responsibilities go both ways, and we all take care of one another because we're a family.

Many of these strategies can be adapted for older children too. Hopefully, older children have already learned some of these lessons about getting outside themselves and seeing things from other people's perspective. Despite their reputation for being self-absorbed, teenagers can certainly understand ethics if you make a point to talk to them. Tell your child about your own ethical decisions. Appeal to his sense of fairness and justice. Encourage him to think logically about challenges he is facing. Try not to start preaching when you're already upset about something. Ideally, you can incorporate ethical concepts into everyday life, like when your child asks you for advice about something or if you see someone else going through a rough time. Don't take it for granted that your child already knows something—talk to him about it. Even if you think he isn't listening, he probably is.

YOU CONTROL YOURSELF, NOT OTHER PEOPLE

This is a tough one to teach to kids. But as we saw with our own parenting philosophy, understanding this concept is essential for happiness. So it's very important to lay the groundwork as early as possible, even if young children can only understand the concept at a rudimentary level. But there is certainly one part of this guideline that everyone can understand: You control yourself.

When Clementine taunts James and he shoves her in retaliation, this rule comes out in full force. "You cannot control what Clementine does, but you can control what *you* do," I tell James. "Even if she says something unkind to you, you are never allowed to push." Or when Clementine claims, "James made me do it," we talk about this concept again. "James can't *make* you do anything," I remind her.

This guideline is also extremely helpful in guiding kids to deal with problems at school. Clementine came home one day and said, "Zoe and Chloe were mean to me today. They said they don't like my new haircut!" Hearing that your child has run into unfriendly playmates is a concern to any parent. And of course, if it is serious or persistent bullying, the problem deserves action from adults. But among four-year-old girls, I think the best strategy is to teach Clementine to stand up for herself without getting upset. Everyone is going to encounter unpleasant people and situations at some point in life. If we can teach our children how to effectively deal with unpleasantness, we will be giving them a wonderful gift.

In this case, I started teaching Clementine that her friends' unkind words are due to *their* flaws, not *her* flaws. "Some children haven't learned how to be nice," I told her. "I know *you* don't say mean things to people, because you already know how to be a good friend. But some other children don't know how to be a good friend." I could see the wheels turning in her head. "If Chloe doesn't know how to be nice, it's not because of your hair—it's because she doesn't know how to be a good friend. Next time that happens, tell her that she shouldn't say mean things. And if she keeps on doing it, tell your teacher."

It's always hard to give good advice, and I certainly don't think there's just one right way to guide kids. But what I hope to show my children is that they don't have to be upset by other people's actions. If they feel sad or mad or frustrated, we can talk about how to work through their feelings and feel better. But when it comes to other people's insults, I think we can teach them from a young age to not feel insulted. We can teach them to stand up for themselves—and for other people who are being treated wrongly—without getting upset.

Remember, the dichotomy of control in no way necessitates passive acceptance of injustices. On the contrary, it is entirely appropriate to take action to defend ourselves and other people. But we can do it without getting angry or feeling offended. That is the key ingredient you want to pass on to your child: Solve the problem without getting upset. (We've come full circle back to the first principle.) You can teach your child that she is not responsible for other people's actions. She is responsible for making sure that she behaves well, but that doesn't mean other people will always behave well.

Learning to control yourself and only yourself is a more advanced idea than the first two we discussed. It requires a certain amount of perspective and understanding that very young children don't have. But you can start planting the seeds early. Wouldn't it be great if your child could grow up without feeling guilty, anxious, or hurt by other people's actions? And if he knew to accept full responsibility for his own behavior? As long as you teach an active version of the dichotomy of control (not a passive doormat version), I think this is a very valuable principle to instill early on. As our kids grow up, we can encourage them to change the things they can and accept the things they cannot change. And we can (hopefully) teach them the wisdom to know the difference.

GIVING CORE PRINCIPLES, NOT INSTRUCTIONS

Now that we've talked about some specific ways to teach your child virtue, let's look at one important guideline for all of your teaching: When possible, give principles instead of instructions. There's a very simple reason for this. As the ancient Stoic writer Seneca puts it, "Instructions will perhaps enable you to do what you ought, but will not guarantee that you do it in the way you should; and if they don't guarantee this they do not lead all the way to virtue. So conviction should be implanted that will affect one's whole life; this is what I call a first principle. Our actions and deliberations will match this conviction; and our life will match these actions."[4]

Let's break down this reasoning. If you try to teach someone how to live virtuously just by providing lots of instructions, you will not succeed. This is because you cannot possibly give someone instructions for every situation he or she will come across in life. Without some other moral foundation, the person will often be at a loss about what to do.

Also, instructions are superficial and are not related to the intentions behind someone's actions. Stoics believe that moral intention is paramount. If you perform a good action but your intention was bad, then it was a bad action on your part. Conversely, if the results of your action happen to be bad but your intention was good, then it was a good action on your part. So the intentions behind our actions are actually more important than the outcome.

Instead of just giving our kids a lot of instructions, we should focus on teaching the basic principles behind the instructions. Seneca even gives us some examples of this. Let's say you want to teach someone to be good to other people. If you teach through instructions, you would have to give her hundreds of instructions: Don't kill people, don't harm people, help survivors of a shipwreck, help survivors of a plane wreck . . . the list would go on forever. But if you teach her the basic principle behind these instructions—that we are all members of the human family and should help one another—then she can apply that one principle to every situation she might encounter in life. Instead of following rote instructions, she will naturally help those in need because she tries to help everyone. Just one principle (helping other people) can replace thousands of individual instructions.

It's kind of like the old saying: "If you *give* someone a fish, he eats for a day. If you *teach* someone to fish, he eats for a lifetime." If you give your child instructions, he is good for a day. If you teach your child virtuous principles, he is good for a lifetime. Well, that's the goal, anyway.

This principle goes hand in hand with talking to your child about virtue. For example, instead of just telling my kids over and over again what to do and what not to do, I try to break down my reasoning for them. So in place of "Don't run so close to Freddy," I try to say, "James, do you want to hurt Freddy? If you run that close to him, you are going to step on him sooner or later. I know you won't mean to hurt him, but you will do it accidentally, and then both of you will feel bad." It might seem obvious to an adult observer that the reason for not running close to Freddy is because he might get hurt, but this is not necessarily obvious to a three-year-old. Explicitly making this logical connection for the child is important.

Yes, it takes about fifteen extra seconds to explain the principle (being nice to others) behind the instruction (don't run so close to Freddy). But once James realizes there is a logical reason for the instructions, not only is he more likely to comply but he is also more likely to remember the rule. And because we talk constantly about being nice to others, he can learn to recognize that this particular instruction is just one iteration of the core principle we follow all the time. The more you explain the core principle, the more the child will start to understand and internalize the core principle for himself. Instead of just receiving a constant stream of disconnected instructions, James can connect the dots and see that all my instructions relate to the same basic principles.

As parents, we are pretty much guaranteed to be giving our kids a lot of instructions, especially when they are young. But I think when we shift our focus from the child's (superficial) behavior to her (moral) intention, we can make our instructions much more effective. By consistently referring to the virtues that guide all our actions, we can help our kids' behavior in both the long and short term. After all, "Instructions are inherently weak and, so to speak, rootless, if they are given for particulars. It is principles which fortify us, which protect our freedom from care and our tranquility, which contain within them all of life and all the universe."[5]

CHAPTER TAKEAWAYS

- Not only can Stoicism teach us how to think clearly, act wisely, and deal with indifferents, but it can also help teach our children the same things.
- Flourishing (or *eudaimonia*, in Greek) can be defined as "the best mindset that is available to human beings." All the other things you might want for your child (such as academic success) can go alongside virtue, but they should not be mistaken as the path to happiness.
- If the path to flourishing is through virtue, as the Stoics suggest, then we have a responsibility to teach our children wisdom, courage, justice, and self-control. Ultimately, it's for their own good.
- To teach kids virtue, talk to them about it all the time and in many different situations. Explain your own moral reasoning to them, and expect them to start applying moral reasoning to their own decisions. This will give your child the vocabulary and concepts to understand virtue for the rest of her life.
- Your child may respond better to correction if it's based on ethical principles rather than parental authority. If you remove your parental ego from the situation—your anxiety, guilt, frustration—you can base your actions entirely on teaching virtue to your child.
- Using Stoic ethical guidelines for our children's behavior is the ultimate technique for clarity and consistency: We are able to teach

them the same core beliefs we use to guide our own behavior. We can teach them to think clearly, act wisely, and deal with indifferents.

- To teach kids how to deal with indifferents, use the reminder *Don't get upset, just deal with the problem.* Help them develop emotional control, deal with frustration, deal with fear or discomfort, and become patient.
- To teach kids how to act wisely, use the reminder *Treat other people the way you want them to treat you.* Help them learn to think about things from another person's perspective. Encourage them to help other people and to be a kind friend or sibling, and remind them that it feels good to be good.
- To teach kids how to think clearly, use the reminder *You control yourself, not other people.* Help them learn to think about their own thoughts and actions. Encourage them to focus on their own behavior, not other people's behavior. Teach them how to calm themselves down and try their best.
- The genius of Stoic psychology is treating the illness (mistaken beliefs) rather than the symptoms (frustration, anger, fear) of negative emotions. If you just treat the symptoms by telling your child to stay calm, then you don't actually change the root cause of the behavior. Instead, try to go straight to your child's value judgment and show him there is no reason to feel frustrated in the first place.
- Whenever possible, try to teach general principles rather than giving surface-level instructions. By teaching principles, you help your child know how to act wisely in a wide variety of situations.

MAKE IT YOUR OWN

- Take a moment to consider what you hope for your child to be, do, and have in life. Do you agree that *eudaimonia* (the lasting, fulfilling, rich happiness that results from a life well lived) is desirable? Do you think there is anything more important than this for your child's life? If there is something better than *eudaimonia*, what is it?
- We cannot actually make our children happy, but we can show them the path to happiness. Where do you believe the path to happiness lies? Do you think the Stoics could be right—that wisdom and virtue lead to flourishing?

- Do you see any advantages to teaching your child wisdom, justice, courage, and self-control? Are there any drawbacks?
- Talking to your child about virtue requires hard work and patience on your part, especially at first. Can you picture yourself doing this? Think through some scenarios in which you respond to your child's misbehavior by explaining your ethical expectations. Try to think about how your child might respond and how you can be as encouraging as possible.
- Take a few minutes to brainstorm ways you can teach virtue at your child's level. What are his interests, likes, and dislikes? Can you explain good behavior in terms of his favorite superhero or story? Can you relate your expectations to a scenario or concept that he is familiar with?
- Look again at the kid-friendly principles we discussed in this chapter. Memorize the basic slogans: Don't get upset, just deal with the problem; treat other people the way you want them to treat you; you control yourself, not other people. Be ready to use them whenever your child could benefit from hearing them.
- Read through the kid-friendly principles and choose one concept you think is most important. Think about ways you could work on that concept with your child. What situations does this concept apply to? How can you explain it effectively to your child? Envision yourself talking about the concept in real life with your child—then do it!
- Think back through the past twenty-four hours with your child. How many times did you give her instructions? Choose one or two of those instances, then identify a way you could convert those instructions into teaching core principles. (It may not be feasible in every situation; sometimes you just have to give plain old instructions. But try to find a time when this would work.) Think about how you would explain those core principles to your child. The next time a similar situation arises, try out this new method of explaining things to him.

6

ENJOYING YOUR CHILD

It was one of those rough days. I picked the kids up from school and we rushed to swim lessons; we got home and everyone was hungry, tired, and cranky. As we walked in the door, Clementine spotted one of her brother's favorite toys lying on the floor. She gleefully grabbed it and hugged it close, turning around to be sure James could see. "Finders keepers!" she squealed with delight. I was just about to launch into a stern lecture when she added, with five-year-old flourish, "Losers squeezers!" I couldn't help it. Despite the gravity of the situation, I started laughing. "It's not losers squeezers, Clementine, it's losers weepers," I told her. "Oh," she said, confused. Then she turned slyly back to James, crowing, "Finders keepers, losers squeakers!"

I'm sure we've all had those moments when we remember why being a parent is an amazing privilege. It might be a surge of pride when your child does something wonderful, or a feeling of overwhelming love as you hold her tight. Or, like my experience with *Losers squeezers*, just a simple reminder that your kids are delightful little people with their own flawed but endearing personalities. In the middle of the daily grind, sometimes you need a reminder that having kids is not just a flurry of activities and obligations—it's a mind-blowing, life-affirming journey with the people you love most in the world.

As we go about our daily lives, with so much to do and so many challenges and interruptions, we sometimes forget to enjoy our children. It can be easy to focus on the difficulties of parenting: the sleep deprivation, the noise, the mess, the expense, the nonstop demands on your attention. It is a truth universally acknowledged that being a parent is hard. But, as I'm sure you know, the good moments more than make up for the bad. Now, what if we could increase those good moments and reduce the difficult ones? What if tranquility parenting could help you truly enjoy your time with your child?

Everything we have talked about in this book is designed to do just that. If you internalize your goals, eliminate negative value judgments, and teach your child virtue with kindness and affection, you will have already made great strides toward tranquility. You will feel less stress, guilt, and frustration in your interactions with your child. You will probably find that you have more mental energy and attention for him. Even if you're just putting on his shoes or taking him to school, you can have high-quality interactions because you are truly focused on being with him.

In this chapter we will talk about some additional ways to be fully present and engaged when you're with your child. Are you surprised that Stoicism has advice on this topic? *Living in the here and now* is another core concept of Stoic philosophy. So is *being happy with what you have* and *keeping things in perspective.* In fact, the Stoics believed that we can only find happiness and fulfillment in the present moment. Therefore, we should cultivate our ability to fully engage in the present. For us as parents, it's important to enjoy our precious and limited time with our children, no matter how many other things we have going on in life.

STOIC MINDFULNESS

Quite often, when I go out somewhere with my three little ones, we run into older adults who look at our family wistfully and say, "Enjoy this time while it lasts. They grow up so fast!" (I'm sure that's never happened to you, right?) I used to feel annoyed at this unwanted advice. In the middle of all the laundry and nose wiping, the days can feel very long rather than very short. But deep down, I know what they mean. The years with your children at home *are* special. It's just hard to pause and enjoy them when you've got so much to do all the time.

So how can we change our perspective and start enjoying our kids more? The ancient Stoics recommended focusing all your energy and attention on the present moment. Not on what you need to get done tomorrow, or what you didn't get done earlier today. Not on your smartphone, your social calendar, or any of those other indifferents that don't really matter for your happiness. Not even on your hopes for the future or your past regrets. Focus on just now—just you and your child.

One modern Stoic, Donald Robertson, calls this state of mental attention Stoic mindfulness. Being mind*ful* is the opposite of being mind*less*.[1] In other words, you are intentionally focusing your attention on something, not just letting your mind be pulled around by whatever is happening around you. If you are able to really focus all your attention on a single point in time—right now—you won't feel like you are being pulled in a thousand different directions. You won't have part of your brain still writing e-mails or fixating on your shopping list. You will be completely immersed in each instant. And you will probably be much happier.

I'm sure you've heard about mindfulness before, and you might think it sounds nice but kind of vague, unrealistic, or unachievable. In a way, that's true. It's not an easy thing to do, especially when you are already short on time and energy. Some days I am just so tired, the last thing I want to do is try to think harder about something. But just like physical exercise, if you can make yourself do it, you will feel great afterward. And just like becoming physically fit, becoming mentally fit will make you healthier and happier in the long run. Plus, the more you practice, the easier it gets. The hardest part is getting started.

Fortunately, incorporating mindfulness into your life is more realistic if you have specific guidance on how to do it. The Stoics offer some useful strategies that can help you engage fully in the present and enjoy your time with your child. In this chapter we will talk about four of these strategies, which I call (1) it's not as bad as you think; (2) wanting what you have; (3) keeping things in perspective; and (4) morning and evening reflection.

IT'S NOT AS BAD AS YOU THINK

As a parent, I constantly find myself wishing things could be different than they actually are. Sometimes it's a wish that my kids weren't so whiny, that my house could magically clean itself, or that it wasn't raining so I could send the kids outside to play. If you have an older child, you might wish that your child made better choices about friends, took school more seriously, or trusted you more. Once we start complaining, there's no shortage of things to complain about.

But my dissatisfaction with the present situation is not going to improve anything. My kids aren't going to radically change overnight; my house is never going to clean itself. So I have a choice: I can continue being dissatisfied and keep wishing for impossible things; or I can decide to be satisfied with what I have, while continuing to rationally work toward a clean house and cooperative children. When I break down my situation in this way, the correct choice seems obvious. It would be foolish to choose constant disappointment over contentment.

So how do you break out of the mental habit of being dissatisfied? In his *Guide to the Good Life*, William Irvine suggests two mental exercises that can help us appreciate what we have: projective visualization and negative visualization. Let's start with projective visualization,[2] which is a little easier because it involves thinking about someone else's life rather than your own. This is what Epictetus, the brilliant Stoic teacher, taught his students:

> When someone else . . . breaks a cup, we're ready at once to say, "That's just one of those things." So you should be clear then, that if your own cup gets broken, you ought to react in exactly the same way as when someone else's does.[3]

Whatever situation you are in, you can be sure that someone else has experienced, or is currently experiencing, the very same thing. This is especially true of us as parents. People have (obviously) been having children since the dawn of humanity. Even though our culture and our technology are different now, our mental experiences are pretty much the same as always. Any frustration or hardship that you are going through now with your child has already been experienced many times by other people.

So imagine that you are a fly on the wall in someone else's home, watching the exact scenario that you happen to find frustrating at the moment. For example, if your child is bouncing off the walls on a cold, rainy afternoon with nothing to do, imagine you are watching another parent deal with the same situation. You don't need to imagine someone you know; just think about an anonymous family you've never met but who has similar children and similar circumstances. They could be living on the other side of town or the other side of the world. They could be living now or at any time in the past. The important thing is that you recognize that the parent in your imaginary scenario feels the exact same thing you are feeling now.

Now that you've seen your imaginary counterpart dealing with a difficult situation, what would you advise her to do? Would you recommend that she get upset, or sad, or angry? As an objective observer, you can probably see that the parent's getting frustrated is not going to help anything. You might even say something like, "Hey, this happens to everyone." What would you recommend that parent should do? Pull out a board game? Sing silly songs for the kids? It helps us to think clearly if we remember that these things happen to everyone and are just a normal part of being a parent.

Sometimes I've had the experience of seeing another parent react badly to a child's behavior and wondering, "Why is she yelling at her kid like that in front of everyone?" When something frustrating happens to someone else, it's easy to see that the best thing is to think clearly and act wisely. (Just try to *learn* from other people's experiences, not judge and criticize.) Then when the same thing happens to us, we forget all that good advice and react badly ourselves. It seems so much worse when it happens to us.

Projective visualization reminds us that it's *not* so much worse when it happens to us. It's the *same*. All parents experience frustrations, annoyances, and challenges with their children. It's false to go around thinking that everyone else has it a lot easier than you do. (Even though their social media feeds might be a constant stream of art projects and trips to the zoo, that's certainly not the reality of their lives. But that's another issue for another day!) In fact, many people might be in situations that are actually a lot harder than yours. No matter how bad your situation is right now, it could always be worse.

WANTING WHAT YOU HAVE

Things are not as bad as we think. Just pausing for a moment to remember that can go a long way toward increasing our satisfaction with life. But there's another type of visualization you can use to become happier.

Negative visualization focuses on wanting what you have rather than trying to get things you want.[4] Believe it or not, appreciating what you have is very closely connected to being fully engaged in the present moment. If you are always wanting more, you are thinking about the future, not the present. But if you truly, fully appreciate what you have in the present moment, you are completely immersed in the here and now. Here is how William Irvine describes the relationship between contentment and the present moment:

> The Stoics argued that the best way to gain satisfaction is not by working to satisfy whatever desires we find within us but by learning to be satisfied with our life as it is—by learning to be happy with whatever we've got. . . . One of the things we've got is this very moment, and we have an important choice with respect to it: We can either spend this moment wishing it could be different, or we can embrace this moment. If we habitually do the former, we will spend much of our life in a state of dissatisfaction; if we habitually do the latter, we will enjoy our life.[5]

Once again, contentment comes down to a choice: Will you be satisfied with what you have right here in the present moment, or pine away for something else? This is a very pressing decision for us as parents because we do not want to squander our valuable time with our little ones. And remember that your children are constantly learning how to live their own lives by watching your behavior. If you are constantly reaching for your phone instead of enjoying the moment with your child, what do you think she will do as she grows up? Your actions set the stage for her actions.

Let's think practically about how you can be happy with what you have. When your child decides not to follow your directions, it's your choice what to think about it. (Remember, our own thoughts and beliefs are one of the few things in life that are truly up to us.) One option is grumbling to yourself, "Why do I have to have such a stubborn child?" When you ask yourself that question, what you really mean is "Why can't I have a perfect child?" or "Why am I the one, out of all the parents in the world, who has to deal with a stubborn child?" But ultimately those are not the right questions to ask. Both questions are based on false assumptions: that there is such a thing as perfection, or that everyone else has it easier than you do.

But what if we looked at that question in a different way? What if you didn't have your child at all? Let's try another thought experiment. Imagine for a moment that you have sent your child on vacation with a family member for a few weeks. At first you'd probably enjoy your time off immensely. You could sleep in on weekends. You would have fewer obligations and demands on your time. You'd have more leisure, more freedom, and probably more cash.

After a few days, though, you would start to miss your child. The house would seem empty. You would start to think about all the fun things you did together, and how much vitality and love your child adds to your life. Sure, you might not have to worry about swim lessons or back talk, but you would miss out on all the new discoveries, all the heartwarming hugs, and all the cute, funny, interesting things your child does every day. You would miss out on the amazing experience of nurturing and loving a remarkable human being. You would miss out on helping him or her become a wonderful young adult, and you wouldn't get to share your life's journey with such a special person. (I'm tearing up just writing it!) Your life would be impoverished if you didn't share it with your child. We usually don't give our kids enough credit for enriching our lives with love and happiness.

That's the point of this thought experiment. Our children might be demanding, but without them life would be much worse. Instead of having a short fuse with our kids, we should appreciate and engage in every moment with them. Being a parent is obviously a huge responsibility, but it is also a huge privilege. We should remember to think of it that way—especially when we're in the middle of a frustrating situation.

By practicing this type of negative visualization from time to time, we can return to our parental obligations with a renewed sense of appreciation for our wonderful kids. Instead of grumbling about their imperfections, we can appreciate that we have them at all. In other words, we love the kids we've got, even though they are not perfect. We choose to be satisfied with what (and who) we have.

KEEPING THINGS IN PERSPECTIVE

Let's go back to the idea of projective visualization that we discussed above. We talked about remembering that other parents are dealing with the same sorts of problems that you are right at this very moment. When it comes to raising kids, every emotion that it's possible to feel has already been felt by many other parents. In the twenty-first century we may have slightly new ways of living, but we do not have new ways of feeling. It's all been done before.

Now let's develop that idea into another psychological exercise that can help you find tranquility with your child. It's called "the view from above" because it asks you to expand your perspective into something much bigger than yourself.[6] First we'll look at how Marcus Aurelius describes this perspective, and then we'll apply it to life as a modern parent. Here's how Marcus advises us to do this exercise:

> One who would converse about human beings should look on all things earthly as though from some point far above, upon herds, armies, and agriculture, marriages and divorces, births and deaths, the clamor of law courts, deserted wastes, alien peoples of every kind, festivals, lamentations, and markets, this intermixture of every-thing. . . . So it is all the same whether you study human life for forty years or ten thousand; for what more can you expect to see?[7]

You can try it out for yourself. Marcus does an excellent job of explaining just how to do it. Close your eyes and imagine being up somewhere very high—you could be in an airplane or standing on a mountaintop, even standing on the moon looking back at Earth. From that perspective, you would see the vastness of the world, with its billions of people, all its plants and animals, and its oceans and forests and ice caps. If you zoomed in a little more, you would see all those people eating breakfast, going on dates, getting sick, telling lies, and doing other things that people always do. Those basic facts of life are repeated by everyone all over the world.

And you would see lots and lots of parents and children. Of those billions of people on the planet, how many of those kids are in the process of misbehaving right now? Probably millions. So then how many are parents feeling exasperated because their kids are misbehaving? Probably millions. Right at this very moment, there are millions of other parents feeling the same as you. Whatever your child is doing, and whatever you yourself are doing, you are in the company of many other people.

That doesn't mean you and your child don't matter. You certainly do matter, and your actions toward your child are very important. This exercise is designed to show you that whatever problems you are dealing with are not yours alone. It can be very easy to feel that you are struggling all alone with your problems and your child. I've certainly felt that way many times before. When you have a child and your life changes radically from what it used to be, you can feel very isolated and marginalized.

But when you take a view from above, you realize that you are not alone at all. Your particular problems, whatever they may be, are common to everyone. If you are lonely, there must be millions (or even billions) of other people who are lonely. If you are stressed, or tired, or frustrated, or sad, or sick—whatever your condition—there are millions of others just like you. That's the reality of being human. Whether your child has problems at school, picks his nose, or doesn't want to participate in family activities, you can be sure there are countless other parents dealing with similar problems. As Marcus says, that's the way things were in the past, and that's the way things will be in the future. Parenting frustrations are part of the natural order of the universe.

I don't know about you, but I find this perspective to be remarkably reassuring. It's not my personal failings as a parent that cause my kids to misbehave sometimes—that's just the nature of things. And my kids are not uniquely frustrating or ill-tempered—there are millions of others like them. There is no need for me to feel guilty or frustrated. Though we do it in different ways, all parents are working toward the same basic goal: to raise good kids and maintain our tranquility while we do it.

MORNING AND EVENING REFLECTION

We've already talked about three helpful mental exercises you can do to refocus your attention on enjoying the present moment. The challenge is finding the time and energy to do them. When you saw the title of this section, "Morning and Evening Reflection," you might have thought, "Yeah, right. Not gonna happen." Parents are the busiest people on Earth. We barely have time to shower every day, much less pause to reflect on our lives. And if you're like me, when you get the kids in bed at night and finally have some downtime, the last thing you want to do is spend more time thinking. Our alone time is limited and valuable. We need to use it wisely.

You might not want someone (like me) telling you what to do with your few moments of daily solitude. All I can tell you is that this has worked for me, and the payoff is worth it. What I'm *not* suggesting is that you add a fifteen-minute meditation session to the end of your day. Instead, it's much more realistic to carve out a time for mental focus during your existing daily routine. If you can find a way to focus your mind for one minute—that's right, only sixty seconds—in the morning and evening, you might find that this works for you.

You could do it while you are drinking coffee, shaving, or possibly commuting (but be careful with that one; you don't want to cause any accidents). You could try to do it while you are lying in bed in the morning and evening. (This is what Seneca recommended, but I have never had much luck with that technique.) What works best for me is to pause and reflect while I'm brushing my teeth in the morning and evening. It's easy to skip a separate meditation session because we're always busy or tired. You always end up telling yourself, "I don't have time right now; I'll do it later." But you have to brush your teeth twice a day. You can't skip it. So why not use that time to focus your mind on tranquility? It's a very short time, but that's OK. If you find that you need more time, you can always add it in. But the main thing is that you do it consistently. Just figure out some part of your schedule where you can add in sixty seconds of focus. Start small, but get started.

What is this morning and evening reflection all about? It's a time to hold yourself accountable for seeking virtue and contentment. It's a time to pause briefly and remember your core beliefs and your parenting philosophy. And it's a time to reflect on whether your interactions with your child match up to your principles.

Both ancient[8] and modern[9] Stoics recommend a specific type of contemplation in the morning and evening. The morning session is designed to help you face the day with tranquility. You prepare yourself to deal with problems so that when problems inevitably arise, you can stay calm and composed. We've discussed this already in chapter 3 in the context of premeditation of adversity. It's all about holding realistic expectations of life. If you expect life to be easy and smooth, you will be disappointed and unprepared for challenges. If you take a realistic view and expect to face challenges, you will be ready to deal with those challenges. You won't be caught off guard, and you won't be disappointed.

As part of tranquility parenting, I recommend that you think about two things during your morning reflection. First, what challenges might you face with your child that day? The easiest thing is to think of issues from the day before. Did he refuse to cooperate? Use inappropriate language? Fudge the truth? Second, think about how you can address that challenge using techniques from this book. (If you're not sure, you might want to check out the reference sections in chapters 9 and 10.) Imagine yourself removing value judgments, focusing on what you can control, and thinking clearly throughout the interaction. Based on your parenting philosophy, how should you correct your child? If you tried a strategy yesterday that didn't work, think about a new strategy to try today.

At the most basic level, this short reflection will remind you to expect problems, and it will remind you of productive ways to solve problems. That will help set the tone for the rest of the day. After you've done this basic exercise, you can keep going if you have time. Donald Robertson suggests choosing "a specific philosophical precept that you want to rehearse" and then "imagining how you could adhere to it more fully during the rest of the day."[10] The philosophical precept you choose could be a particular virtue, such as courage or self-control. Or it could be a mental technique to really work on that day: keeping things in perspective, wanting what you have, focusing on what you can control, etc. You could even choose an aspect of our tranquility parenting philosophy—thinking clearly, acting wisely, or dealing with indifferents— you think would be helpful that day.

In the evening it will be time to review how much progress you made. Remember, no one is perfect, so you shouldn't beat yourself up if you made a few mistakes. The important thing is that you are trying. If you didn't do as well as you hoped that day, you can try again tomorrow. When you do your evening reflection, you will probably want to think about these three things: one thing you did well with your child, one thing you didn't do well, and how you can improve for the next day. If you lost your temper with your child, think about what mental techniques you can use to be calmer. And when you do your reflection the next morning, pick up on that same technique to practice during the day.[11]

Don't try to do too much at once. Earlier I compared mindfulness to physical exercise, and I think the analogy is even more useful here. When you start a physical training program, you don't immediately try to go out and run a marathon or bench-press three hundred pounds. You start small and work your way up. If you do too much too fast, you will probably get injured and demoralized. If you expect to become a marathoner overnight, you will be disappointed and feel bad about yourself. It's important to have realistic expectations about what you can accomplish.

It's the same for building Stoic mindfulness. If you start with reasonable expectations, you won't get upset and give up. Don't expect to become a sage, and don't tell yourself that you will spend half an hour in studious contemplation every night. That's probably not realistic. Instead, carve out time when you can. Don't expect conditions to be perfect; you don't need perfect stillness and beautiful birdsong and incense. Just start doing it when and how you can. Even a couple minutes a day is much better than nothing.

And try to be honest but forgiving as you review the day's activities. I draw inspiration from Seneca, who was a famous but flawed Stoic philosopher. Here's how he described his evening meditation:

> I examine the whole of my day and retrace my actions and words; I hide nothing from myself, pass over nothing. For why should I be afraid of any of my mistakes, when I can say: "Beware of doing that again, and this time I pardon you."[12]

In other words, you are not doing this exercise to feel guilty. You're only human. Pardon yourself for any mistakes, and think about how you can do better tomorrow.

Remember to be specific when you think about areas for improvement. I find it fascinating that Seneca's advice to himself closely resembles what we, as parents, might need to work on. He tells himself, "In that discussion you spoke too aggressively: Do not, after this, clash with people of no experience," or "You were more outspoken in criticizing that man than you should have been, and so you offended, rather than improved him."[13] I think many parents can relate to these flaws. We still have trouble keeping our temper and offering gentle correction. Just like we said earlier, everything that *can* be felt has *already been* felt. That's why these ancient Stoic mental techniques are as useful today as ever.

What about those reflections we talked about earlier in the chapter, like projective and negative visualization and the view from above? You might want to try those as coping strategies when you feel your irritation rising. You could pause for a moment and remind yourself to keep things in perspective, or practice projective visualization. But if you're able to, you could also set aside a few minutes every week to do these extra reflections. Do you have five minutes, maybe sometime over the weekend, to do some additional concentration? If you can fit it in, you'll probably find it very rewarding. The more you can practice mindfulness, the closer you will get to tranquility.

CHAPTER TAKEAWAYS

- In the middle of all our daily obligations and challenges, we sometimes forget to enjoy our children. Part of tranquility parenting is making the most of every moment with your child and learning to truly appreciate what you have.
- Stoic mindfulness means intentionally focusing your mental energy on the present moment. Be aware of what is going through your mind right now, and then learn to direct it in a fulfilling direction.
- Mindfulness is easier to accomplish if you have specific strategies to guide you. In this chapter we talk about four strategies: (1) It's not as bad as you think; (2) wanting what you have; (3) keeping things in perspective; and (4) morning and evening reflection.
- To change from being dissatisfied to being content, remember that things are not as bad as you think, and that it's best to be happy with what you have. Negative and projective visualization can help us do this.
- As part of projective visualization, you think about another parent who has the exact same problem you do. Problems seem less severe and easier to handle when they happen to other people. Think about what advice you would give to that other parent.

- As part of negative visualization, you imagine that you could no longer see your child every day. We usually don't give our kids enough credit for enriching our lives with love and happiness. By pausing to consider life *without* your child, you can fully appreciate life *with* your child.
- Try to keep things in perspective by imagining the view from above. Zoom out for a moment and imagine the millions of other parents—past, present, and future—who have dealt with child misbehavior. You are not alone! It happens to everyone.
- When you look at the big picture of parenting, you remember that all children misbehave sometimes. As long as you're doing your best, there's no need to feel guilty or frustrated.
- Try to carve out time for a brief reflection during your morning and evening routine. You don't need to wait for the perfect time, because that will never come. Just take anything you can get. The important thing is to get started and do it consistently.
- During your morning reflection, try to think about two things: (1) What challenges might you face with your child that day? (2) How can you address that challenge effectively? If you have extra time, you can reflect on a virtue or mental technique that you want to practice that day.
- During your evening reflection, try to think about three things: (1) one thing you did well with your child; (2) one thing you didn't do well; and (3) how you can improve for the next day.
- Don't beat yourself up for not handling every challenge perfectly. The purpose of meditation is not to feel bad about yourself but to figure out how to improve. Be honest with yourself about your shortcomings, but also forgive yourself and move on.
- Hold realistic expectations about what you can accomplish with meditation. It's like starting a physical fitness program. Start small and work your way up slowly. Don't expect too much at once.

MAKE IT YOUR OWN

- Think about a time in the past when you managed to feel fully present and engaged with your child. What led you to the experience? How did you feel? Would you like to repeat that experience more often?

- Do you tend to be dissatisfied with yourself, your life, or your child? Make a list of five to ten things you have been dissatisfied with recently. These items will be the raw material you work on as we go through the four strategies for contentment below.

- It's not as bad as you think. Think back to a difficult situation with your child. Now imagine that the same thing happened to another parent you know (real or fictitious). If that parent came to you for advice, what would you tell him or her? Would you advise that parent to stay calm and keep things in perspective? What strategies would you recommend to deal with the problem? Now turn that advice around toward yourself. Can you implement that advice in your own life?

- Wanting what you have. Try out the negative visualization exercise in this chapter. What goes through your mind when you think about life without your child versus life with your child? Does life with your child suddenly seem wonderful and meaningful, even if it is a bit chaotic?

- Keeping things in perspective. Try the "view from above" exercise suggested by Marcus Aurelius. As you look over the whole world, do you see how much company you have in dealing with parenting problems? We can still try to improve ourselves and our kids, but we should remember that some experiences are just a part of life.

- Think through your daily routine and identify a sixty-second period in the morning and evening when you can do a brief meditation. Do whatever it takes to make yourself focus during this time: Put up sticky notes by your mirror; set a reminder on your phone; make a schedule to force yourself to do it. And why not give yourself a little reward when you manage to stick with it?

- You might want to check in with yourself on a weekly basis to see how the meditation routine is going. How is it working out? Maybe you need to pick a different time or read through another section of this book for more ideas on handling challenges. Are the strategies you selected working out? If they aren't, feel free to change them. It's all about trial and error. Figure out what works for you and your family. Just don't give up!

7

OVERCOMING YOUR ANXIETY

Some parents are blessed with an innate ability not to worry about their kids. (Maybe they are just natural Stoics.) Unfortunately, I am not one of them. Even before my daughter was born, I found plenty of things to worry about. Is the car seat installed properly? Is baby powder harmful? Will store-bought baby food establish bad eating habits for the rest of her life? Even the things that were supposed to be safe and helpful were fraught with peril.

These fears were not completely my fault. My natural anxiety was compounded by the culture of worry surrounding childhood and parenting. I didn't just make up things to worry about—I read about them. I had no idea so many things could go wrong until I picked up a parenting magazine at a maternity appointment. Suddenly, raising a child sounded terrifying. I was sure I would break some hidden rule, unknowingly putting my baby in grave danger. After Clementine was born, I was so worried about her that I couldn't relax. My heart was full of love, but I felt that it was beating mostly out of anxiety.

Five years and two more children later, I am happy to say that some of this anxiety eased naturally as I learned how to take care of my kids. I figured out how to do things safely, and experience taught me that the risk of most dangers is actually quite small. But what really helped diminish my constant worry is Stoic philosophy. Fear and anxiety are some of the negative emotions that Stoicism helps eliminate. In this chapter we will talk about how to deploy Stoic principles to overcome one of the most natural fears in the world: worry about your child.

I'm not saying it's easy. If you tend to worry, it takes a lot of mental work to reduce your unease. And yet, in this book we've already talked about everything you need to know. All the Stoic principles we've discussed so far can help. Now we just have to apply them specifically to the area of fear and anxiety.

Before we get started, I'd like to remind you that this book is intended for parents who have normal fears for the safety of their child, not for those who have clinical anxiety. I am not using the terms "anxiety," "worry," and "fear" in the same way a therapist would. Tranquility parenting does not replace the guidance of a therapist. If you believe you may be suffering from clinical anxiety, please see a mental health professional.[1] If you just tend to worry sometimes about your child, read on for some strategies that might help you deal with those worries.

REPAIRING YOUR VALUE JUDGMENTS

As Roman emperor, Marcus Aurelius was the most powerful man on Earth. That's why it's so touching to read his personal reflections on topics that we all must face: putting up with other people; striving to be good in a world that doesn't understand you; the temptations of money and status; the impermanence of material things. His philosophical reflections are a poignant reminder that no matter how rich and powerful you are, you are still just a person.

In his *Meditations*, Marcus clearly grapples with anxiety about his children's health. Consider, for example, the following passage on value judgments: "Say nothing more to yourself than what the first impressions report. You have been told that some person is speaking ill of you? That is what you have been told: as to the further point, that he has harmed you, that you have not been told."[2] You could read this (as we did in chapter 3) as a straightforward explanation of eliminating negative value judgments. But then Marcus goes on to say, "I see that my little child is ill? I just see that; I do not see that his life is at risk. And so in this way, always keep to first impressions."

In other words, Marcus is using the same mental technique—eliminating false value judgments—to overcome anxiety about his children. It's very touching that in the emperor's most private thoughts, he struggled with the same worries we still feel almost two millennia later. And it offers us hope that if he found a way to cope, we can find the courage to overcome our own anxieties.

At first glance, it might not seem obvious how different emotions like anger, frustration, fear, and anxiety are connected. But remember, Stoicism teaches that all negative emotions result from mistaken beliefs about the world. You will feel insulted only if you believe that someone else has the power to insult you. If you change your beliefs, you also change your emotions. So if this strategy can help you deal with insults and frustrations, can it also help you stop worrying about your kids?

Let's think again about the process of forming an impression. Remember, this is one way the Stoics describe the "uneducated" way of looking at the world:[3]

1. We perceive an external object or situation.
2. We interpret the event to ourselves by combining sensory information, prior experience, existing attitudes, etc.
3. We create a value judgment about the impression.

Those value judgments might seem like they are an integral part of the impression, or that they are inseparable from the raw sensory information we receive about the world. But the value judgment is really just an opinion that you add on to the sensory information. It is not an objective truth. If you eliminate or change the false judgment, you are not distorting your view of reality. In fact, you are bringing your mental processes more in line with reality.

Before I adopted a Stoic approach to life, I saw everything in the world as a potential threat to my children. And if something was a threat, I had to be constantly on the lookout for harm. Cars, fevers, food, playgrounds, and pretty much everything else raised alarm bells in my mind. The problem with this way of seeing the world is not that it is false, but that it is not the whole picture. Yes, there is a small possibility that any of those things could harm my child. But should I let that remote possibility guide my thoughts and behavior?

When you worry too much, it means you are making the wrong value judgment about a situation. Let's say your child comes down with a fever, for example. This is what my old, anxiety-filled thought process looked like:

1. **Perception:** Freddy's temperature is 102.

2. **Interpretation:** Freddy has a fever.
3. **Value judgment:** Freddy's life is in danger.

As you can see, my perception and interpretation in this situation were completely accurate. Freddy's temperature was an objective fact, and a fever in children is objectively defined as core body temperature above 100.4 degrees Fahrenheit. But the value judgment was simply my opinion, based on all the scary stories I'd read and my natural tendency to worry. The idea that Freddy was in danger was my own judgment of how dangerous this situation was. After all, some parents don't start biting their nails the minute their child gets a fever (and they love their child just as much as I love mine). They simply have a different judgment of the situation.

Just like we've seen before, we can reduce negative emotions by getting rid of the false negative assumption we add to our impressions. Just because my child has a fever does not mean his life is in danger. And it does not mean I have to start worrying. As Marcus reminds himself, "I see that my little child is ill? I just see that; I do not see that his life is at risk." I see that Freddy has a fever, but I do not need to start imagining all the terrible things that might possibly happen.

Here's what a more productive way of thinking might look like:

1. **Perception:** Freddy's temperature is 102.
2. **Interpretation:** Freddy has a fever.
3. **Decision:** I should stay calm, make Freddy comfortable, and keep an eye out for other symptoms.
4. **Reaction:** Give Freddy some extra care; review our doctor's advice on dealing with fevers.

I can still make a rational decision to keep an eye out for anything worrisome, *while not worrying about it myself*. I'm certainly not advising you to be cavalier and not care about your child's health. We should always take reasonable precautions. But it's all about your approach. If you sit around expecting something bad to happen, you are adopting a false view of the situation. That is not healthy for you or your child. If you instead take a wait-and-see approach, you can calmly try to make the situation better without fretting. You can focus on what is in your control, like bringing the fever down and helping your child rest. You can inform yourself about the risks without *worrying* about them. In any case, it's not like you're going to make things worse by staying calm and thinking clearly.

Obviously, the purpose of this mental technique is not to make you ignore real dangers to your child. The purpose is to change how you *react* to those dangers. You can still be an attentive and protective parent, but you should hold a realistic view of the situation, not an alarmist view. As William Irvine suggests in *A Guide to the Good Life*,[4] you might think of it as being a meteorologist studying weather patterns. A meteorologist carefully looks at all the available information and keeps an eye out for tornadoes and other hazards. But that doesn't mean she thinks a tornado is about to come after her.

We all have to find the best response to the available information. We get a lot of information about the many things that could harm our children, but we need to filter it through the right thought processes. Caution is a reasonable response; worry is not. Try to repair your value judgments by focusing on what is objectively true. In other words, don't jump to conclusions—just focus on the facts and on what you can do to help.

FOCUSING ON WHAT YOU CAN CONTROL

In chapter 2, I mentioned that the dichotomy of control is probably the most essential concept in tranquility parenting. When you use it to deal with everyday parenting challenges, you eliminate a lot of frustration, guilt, confusion, and anger. That in itself would be enough to rank the dichotomy of control as probably the greatest parenting tool ever. But in addition to all that, the Stoic dichotomy can also help release you from the grip of worry and fear about your child. Once you stop worrying about things you cannot control, you eliminate most of the worry in your life. That frees up a lot of mental and emotional space for you to focus on what you *can* control: parenting to the best of your ability.

Let's review the dichotomy of control, which was updated by the modern Stoic William Irvine into the trichotomy of control.[5] There are some things in life we have complete control over: our own beliefs, attitudes, and actions. There are some things we have no control over whatsoever: the weather, the economy, most of what other people do.

Then there are some things we may be able to influence in some way but don't actually control. Our children fall into this third category.

As much as we would like to, we don't get to choose what happens to our kids. We don't control what accidents happen to them, how other people treat them, or whether, after all our hard work, they ever do find the path to true happiness. You could spend every minute of every day worrying about her, but it would still do nothing to improve your child's chance of having a good life. It might even make things worse.

If we try to control things we cannot actually control, we will be frustrated and miserable. That's why trying to completely control your child is always a bad idea. Once you acknowledge this, you start to focus on what you *can* do. And what you can do is use whatever tools are available to help your child develop into a good, healthy, happy person.

Remember our philosophy of tranquility parenting: thinking clearly, acting wisely, and dealing with indifferents. This is the perfect time to remember these three steps. A complete philosophy of life and philosophy of parenting should be able to cover every situation, ranging from the mildly annoying to the very serious. Just as Marcus uses the same techniques to deal with both insults and anxiety, we can use the coping strategies from chapter 2 in anxiety-provoking situations. Those two strategies are internalizing your goals and focusing on input rather than output. Now we can apply them here.

When you internalize your goals, you change your goal from *preventing any accidents* to *doing my best to prevent any accidents*. Achieving the first goal is impossible. There is no way you will prevent all accidents and injuries in your child's life. So prevent what you can, but accept that sometimes your child is going to get hurt.

Once you accept this reality, you can shift your focus from fear to coping. For example, you can handle your child's infirmities by staying calm and taking appropriate action to help him recover. Remember to keep your goals internal, not external. If your child gets hurt, your goal is not *making Freddy better* (because that is outside your control) but rather *helping Freddy to get better* (which is within your control). You can't physically heal your child, but you can take steps to keep him comfortable and speed up his recovery as much as possible.

Internalizing your goals has two important benefits in a situation like this. First, you change your goal from something impossible to something possible, so you actually have a chance of succeeding. Second, you drop the anxious part of your mind out of the equation. Worry has no place in the goal *helping Freddy to get better*. Being an attentive and helpful parent *does* contribute to Freddy's well-being; being a worried and anxious parent *does not*. If you keep your mind focused on your goal of helping, then you should only do things that actually help.

The other strategy we discussed in chapter 2 is focusing on your own input. You don't control the outcome of the situation, but you do control your opinion, motivation, desires, aversions, and actions. Try to think carefully about your opinion of the situation. Is it accurate? If you hold false opinions about how dangerous a situation is, or about how much control you have, then repair your false value judgment. Are you feeling guilty that you can't prevent every accident, illness, and discomfort in your child's life? That is an impossible goal. You will always feel anxious and guilty if you believe your role is to prevent your child from ever experiencing hardship. So be sure your motivations and desires are realistic. You can never eliminate all risk in your child's life, but you can be a caring parent who takes reasonable precautions and faces problems as cheerfully as possible.

BEING COURAGEOUS AND TEACHING COURAGE

At the beginning of this book, we talked about the characteristics of an ideal parent. Let's take another look at this concept, because having an ideal, or role model, can be a very useful guide when we need help.[6] So take a minute to think about your ideal parent. It doesn't have to be someone you know, or even someone real. It could be a fictional character or just an imaginary ideal based on characteristics you value. Describe his or her specific characteristics to yourself. Is that person calm, kind, wise, and witty, even when dealing with challenges? Is he cool and unruffled in the midst of disappointments and difficulties? Does she know when to stop worrying about her child? Can she teach her child to be brave?

I think we would probably all agree that an ideal parent is courageous. She would not spend time worrying about things she can't control, and she wouldn't hover over her child trying to prevent every accident or hardship. She would probably recognize that hardships actually make her child more resilient, persistent, and resourceful. She would accept that some bad things are bound to happen at some point. Instead of investing all her energy in worrying, she would prepare herself and her family to deal with those potential challenges.

The thing about raising kids is that we know for sure we can't protect them from all the undesirable facts of life. It takes a wise person to know when to put away the bubble wrap and start teaching resilience. How can imagining an ideal parent help us in real life? It can give you something to aim for.[7] If you realize that you are worried about your child's safety or behavior, picture your ideal parent dealing with the same situation. If her child were doing the same thing yours is, what would she feel? How would she react? Try to do and say the same thing you think she would. Would she use some of our tranquility parenting strategies to stay calm? Would she focus on what she can control and eliminate false value judgments? Then you do the same.

Remember, worrying doesn't make you a good parent. It's tempting to consider ourselves more involved or better parents because we spend a lot of energy fretting about our kids' future. But that assumption doesn't stand up to logic. You are a good parent because you love your child and invest your time and energy in caring for your child. That doesn't involve worry. You would still be just as good a parent if you converted that worry into a more productive form of care, such as being fully present and appreciating your child. Remember to think clearly about what you are really doing. Your time and mental energy are precious resources, and you don't want to waste them. You want to apply them wisely so that you can be a happy and effective parent.

Think of it this way: When your child grows up and looks back on his childhood, how do you want him to remember you? As an anxious and overprotective parent, or as someone who recognized the inherent uncertainties in life but faced them courageously? As someone who taught him to be fearful of the world, or as someone who taught him how to handle challenges and difficulties? You can be 100 percent sure that your child will face some problems in life, including some physical and emotional pain. There is no getting around it. Do you want to prepare him to face these challenges well or badly? What sort of person do you want him to become?

Remember, you not only have your own role models but are also a de facto role model for your child. He will certainly have memories of how you behaved in various situations. And he will use those memories (maybe unconsciously) to orient himself toward or away from certain actions and ways of living. If you're a positive role model, he will be more likely to behave in the same way. And when you look back, you will know you did your best to set a courageous example for your child.

TURNING YOUR MENTAL ACTIVITY TO YOUR ADVANTAGE

If you're prone to worrying, you probably have an overactive brain that just won't shut off. You might tell yourself to relax, you might try meditation or yoga, you might drink chamomile tea or breathe deeply when you feel anxious. And despite all that, you might still worry a little about your child. You might have a nagging feeling that you haven't covered all the bases. There are so many things that could go wrong—her health, her school, her friends, her sports, her entire future.

I used to be very frustrated that I couldn't make myself relax, and especially that I couldn't make myself sleep. I should be able to control my own mind, I told myself. Why can't I just turn it off, or at least clear my thoughts for a few hours? All the meditation techniques I tried said to make your mind empty or to focus on your breathing, your body, or your surroundings. It didn't work for me. I just couldn't clear my mind. It only made me feel worse about myself.

When I started reading about Stoic mental techniques, I had the sudden, wonderful realization that I didn't need to shut my mind off—I just needed to turn my bad thoughts into good ones. In fact, having an overactive brain could actually be a good thing in Stoicism, because living your ideals requires a lot of thinking. But instead of thinking anxious thoughts, I could think about wisdom and excellence. Perfect! There was no need to turn off my brain. I just had to figure out how to orient my thoughts in the right direction.

I'm pretty sure that if I could do it, anyone can. One of the reasons tranquility parenting has helped me so much is that I started out with so many negative emotions. I think (maybe?) there are some people out there who really don't have anxiety, guilt, frustration, and insecurity about their children. But those people probably couldn't write a book on tranquility. If it comes naturally to them, they may not need specific mental techniques to stay calm. For me, on the other hand, tranquility is hard-won. I've had to completely turn my mind around, and I've had to use very conscious and specific techniques to do it. In some ways I'm still working on it, and I will probably be working on it for the rest of my life. But at least I know these methods can work even for people who start out with a lot of negative emotions.

So now all you need to do is rewire your brain. Piece of cake, right? To start with, you have to think about your thinking. When you notice yourself starting to have anxious or unproductive thoughts, switch to a different train of thought. I visualize my thoughts as a train driving down a track. (In my version it's one of those old-fashioned steam locomotives, and at the very last second it gets switched to a different track, like Road Runner playing a trick on Wile E. Coyote. Who says you can't keep a sense of humor with this?) But in order to switch your thoughts away from a negative direction, you must find a positive direction to move toward. What should that positive direction be?

Choose a positive mantra. I started with a very simple one: *Some things are up to me and some things are not.* Whenever I noticed my thoughts going in a bad direction, I just started repeating that phrase to myself over and over. Again, it's like exercise. When you start out, it takes a lot of effort and you may not be very good at it. You just have to get started. Once you get started, you can build up bit by bit as you're ready.

You can pick whatever mantra or key words you want. It could be a variation of Stoic ideas or your core principles: Be happy with what you have; change what you can and accept the rest; be patient with yourself and everyone else. It could be a song lyric, a religious verse, or anything that gives you strength and inspiration.

The important thing is that you pick something, and that you switch it on in your brain whenever your thoughts turn anxious. Just repeat it to yourself as long as it takes to start thinking about something different. If your thoughts return to your anxiety, go back to your mantra. You are working to build new connections in your brain. The neural path to worry and fear has been engraved in your mind so frequently that it gets switched on very easily. You have to establish new pathways. It doesn't really matter what that new pathway is, as long as you train yourself to go down a more positive path instead of indulging your anxiety.

If you let your thoughts run in any direction they want, Epictetus says, they will lead you on, take possession of you, and conduct you wherever they want.[8] In other words, you will become a captive to your negative thoughts. Doesn't that sound like the experience of anxiety? If you allow yourself to be captured by anxious thoughts, you often have the same dreadful scenarios playing themselves out in your head over and over again. You become a prisoner of your anxiety. In order to keep control of our minds, Epictetus says, we should replace our negative, false impressions with a "fine and noble impression."[9] In other words, we should remove the negative part of our impression and substitute a beautiful thought instead. This is where the mantra comes in.

Your beautiful thought—your mantra—can help you "overpower your impression and not be swept away by it."[10] In fact, Epictetus uses very strong language to describe this process of wrestling with your impressions. It is an epic struggle, like an Olympic contest, a battle, or a storm at sea. "Here is the true athlete, one who trains himself to confront such impressions! Hold firm, poor man, don't allow yourself to be carried away. Great is the struggle, and divine the enterprise, to win a kingdom, to win freedom, to win happiness, to win peace of mind."[11]

The struggle against impressions may be difficult, but the rewards are great. So the next time you feel your heart start to seize up about your child's well-being, grab that anxious thought and throw it aside. Have a mantra or some positive phrase waiting in your mind so that you can immediately focus on a beautiful and peaceful thought. Remember that your feeling of fear is just an opinion, which means you can change it. Remember how much courage it takes to be a parent, and think about what you want to teach your child. Then celebrate each small victory—and be prepared for a long battle. Peace of mind takes a lot of work, but each of us is fully equipped to achieve it. The important thing is to start working now.

CHAPTER TAKEAWAYS

- Just as we used Stoic psychology to reduce anger, frustration, and stress, we can use Stoic psychology to reduce anxiety, worry, and fear.
- When you worry too much, it means you are making the wrong value judgment about a situation. To repair your judgments, remove the

false value judgment and replace it with a productive decision and reaction.

- We hear a lot of information about the many things that could harm our children, but we need to filter it through the right thought processes. Caution is a reasonable response; worry is not. Try to repair your value judgments by focusing on what is objectively true.
- When dealing with a potentially dangerous situation, focus on what you can control. You can't control what happens to your child. Once you acknowledge this, you start to focus on what you *can* do.
- Internalize your goals and focus on your own input into the situation. This allows you to take action in a way that will actually help your child rather than wasting your energy on unproductive worry.
- Visualize a wise and courageous ideal parent. If that person were in your situation, what would he do? Try to imagine his thoughts and actions, then do those same things.
- You are a role model for your child. When she grows up and looks back at her childhood, do you want her to remember you as hovering and anxious? Or would you prefer to be remembered as strong and wise?
- It is 100 percent guaranteed that your child is going to experience pain, disappointment, and problems in life. Think about how you can teach him to deal courageously with the inherent challenges of living.
- If you have an overactive brain, try to channel your mental activity in the right direction. Work toward building new mental habits by replacing your anxious thoughts with beautiful thoughts.
- Find a positive mantra that you find meaningful and useful. When your thoughts start going in a negative direction, switch your train of thought over to the new mantra. Keep repeating it for as long as necessary until your thoughts can move on to something else (away from your anxiety).
- Rewiring your brain takes time and patience. Start small. Take control of your thoughts one time per day. Then two times per day. Work your way up, and celebrate each victory. If you backslide, just start over. Remember that you are taking part in an epic struggle, but the rewards are tranquility and peace of mind.

MAKE IT YOUR OWN

- What things do you worry about? Spend a day or two noticing your own worries. Sometimes we are not even aware of what we are doing! Try to pinpoint the sources of your worry and make yourself consciously aware of them.
- Choose one of your worries and carefully examine it. Why are you worried about this particular issue? (Have you had a bad experience with it before? Did you see it on TV?) What are the actual risks to your child? Is there any way you can completely eliminate this problem from your child's life, or is it something he will always have to live with? What is a reasonable response to this challenge?
- Think about your greatest worry or fear for your child. Break it down just like we did earlier in this chapter: perception, interpretation, value judgment. Now remove the value judgment and write down a reasonable decision and reaction. Whenever you start to worry, replace your judgment with a decision and reaction.
- If you have a persistent worry or fear, make a list of all the possible factors that could influence the situation. Make three columns: one for factors you can completely control, one for factors you have no control over, and one for factors you can influence. Choose the factors you should focus on. Come up with an action plan for yourself based only on those factors you can control.
- It's time to choose your mantra! For me, the most useful one was *Some things are up to me, and some things are not.* But I encourage you to spend some time thinking about what your go-to phrase will be. It could be a song lyric, a religious verse, or anything that gives you strength and inspiration. Just be sure it's short and memorable, because you are going to be repeating it to yourself a lot.
- If it helps, keep a tally of how often you use these psychological tools to change your thoughts. This is a good system to (1) figure out how often you worry and (2) learn which techniques help you the most. Try out all the techniques from this chapter. Notice which ones are most useful for you and become really good at using them.
- Set up a reward system for yourself. For example, if you tally five times that you changed your train of thought from negative to positive, give yourself a pat on the back. If you go a whole day without worrying, congratulate yourself for making progress.

8

FINDING TRANQUILITY

In this book we have talked a lot about *thinking*. I have used words like reason, rationality, thought processes, mental habits, value judgments, inner discourse, reflection, mindfulness, and, of course, wisdom. By this point you might be tired of thinking. You might just want a break from all the hard work of controlling your mind. Believe me, I've been there too.

You might also be wondering if maybe it's not too much thinking and too little feeling. Parenting is basically about loving your child, right? Shouldn't love play an important role in tranquility parenting?

It certainly does. Love plays a central role in everything you do as a parent, especially in thinking clearly, acting wisely, and dealing with indifferents. Love is not something separate—it is a part of every thought and every action as a parent. The more you learn to be calm, mindful, and engaged, the greater your capacity to love your child. By eliminating your negative emotions, you free up more energy to sincerely love and appreciate her.

All that thinking definitely takes hard work, but once you learn how to use good judgment in parenting, the rewards are truly great. As I've said from the beginning of the book, the Stoics did not aim to eliminate all feelings, just the negative emotions that result from seeing things in the wrong way. There are some emotions we should actually cultivate, such as enjoyment, cheerfulness, good spirits, goodwill, cherishing, and selfless love.[1] If you become wise, Seneca says, you will be "cheerful, calm, and undisturbed," and you will live "on equal terms with the gods."[2] Yes, please! Sign me up. I don't mind some difficult mental training if that's what awaits at the end of the road.

Best of all, you have the chance to bring your child along with you. Even though you cannot control what your child does, you can do your best to teach her how to work toward flourishing and tranquility. She is much more likely to find happiness herself if you show her how it's done. However, please do not feel guilty for not instantly becoming a paragon of virtue. This is a lofty ideal to work toward, and it takes a lifetime to achieve. Right here, in the present, it's more about where your priorities are and what path you have chosen. As long as you are trying to move in the right direction, you are still helping your child find that path for herself.

Let's wrap up part one of this book with a few tranquility-related reminders. First, we'll talk about the important role of love in Stoicism and tranquility parenting. Next, we'll look at a few more positive emotions that Stoicism can help us develop. Finally, we'll consider how to integrate tranquility parenting and positive emotions into everyday life. When we're done, I hope you'll be able to truly apply these Stoic principles to your real life as a parent. I'm confident that all the hard work you've been doing will soon start to pay off.

THE IMPORTANT ROLE OF LOVE

The ancient Stoics strongly believed in love. They thought that the natural affection parents have for their children is one of the most obvious and important bonds available to humans. We are inherently social creatures who are meant to cooperate and love one another. If you need proof of this, said Epictetus, just look at how we are hardwired to love and care for our children. "As soon as one has a small child," he says, "it's no longer in our power not to love it and take care of it."[3] It is part of our nature to love our children. In fact, parental love is so powerful and necessary, it can teach us how to love everyone else in the world too.[4]

But when we use the word "love" in Stoic philosophy, we don't mean a passionate, Romeo-and-Juliet type of love that leads people to do foolish things. We are talking about a pure, rational kind of love that wishes for true happiness for others. We don't want to be blinded by love; we want to be made wiser through love. Loving someone in a wise way does not mean our love is weak, insincere, or somehow not real.

Actually, the opposite is true. By becoming more virtuous, we can love more truly and powerfully. Both Gaius Musonius Rufus[5] and Epictetus[6] insist that understanding philosophy will help parents love their children on a deeper level. Or as the modern Stoic teacher Donald Robertson puts it, "Our natural affection for those close to us is not *eliminated* by Stoicism but rather expanded, and transformed in accord with wisdom and virtue."[7] When we have a greater capacity for wisdom, we also have a greater capacity for love.

So if you love your child truly and deeply, how do you act? How do you express your love? From a Stoic perspective, parental affection reveals itself in two main activities: acting virtuously yourself, and teaching your child virtue. We've talked about both activities throughout this book; we've even discussed the reason virtue is so important. It's the path to *eudaimonia*, which is absolute flourishing and happiness. Maybe the ultimate expression of love is helping your child find this path. You can never force anyone to become happy and flourish, but you can always show him or her the way.

THE GOOD EMOTIONS

Let's say all your mental hard work pays off and you find yourself enjoying tranquility, peace of mind, and contentment. You've eliminated negative emotions such as anger, frustration, and fear. You are no longer upset by your child's behavior or anyone else's criticism. You do your best to live wisely and guide your child toward virtue. Then what do you actually feel? Are your emotions feeble, like fluttery shadows? Are you emotionless like a statue or a stone?

Not at all. Unfortunately, I can't speak from personal experience, because I have not reached this perfected state (and probably never will). But Stoic philosophy does have an answer. Once you reach *eudaimonia*, you feel continuous joy and goodwill. Your emotions are not weak or watered down—in fact, they are stronger and unconquerable. "Gladness is torn apart for those who are still undeveloped," according to Seneca, "but the joy of the wise man is firmly woven, it is not torn by any issue or fortune; he is always and everywhere calm."[8] You no longer depend on external circumstances for happiness but rather on your own understanding of life.

If you manage to prune away all your negative emotions, you have much more mental space for the positive ones. Having more space for joy means you can find enjoyment in spending time with your child, or in whatever else you're doing at the moment. You can feel constantly cheerful, because you know that you are doing your best to be wise, kind, courageous, and fair, no matter what anyone else is doing. And you can be in good spirits, which is another way of saying that all is well with the world. You won't be disturbed by anything that happens around you.

I hope it has become clear that the end point of Stoicism is not to become stony-faced or emotionless but to become emotionally invincible and perfectly happy. We may never reach that perfect end point, but we can at least make progress. And best of all, we can bring our children with us on the journey. I like the way Donald Robertson puts it in *Stoicism and the Art of Happiness*: "Love entails a benevolent wish for others to flourish naturally, like a ripening fruit, and to attain Happiness in accord with virtue."[9] If we find a bit of tranquility for ourselves and at the same time help our children "ripen" into a flourishing life, that's a job well done.

AN INTEGRATED PHILOSOPHY OF LIFE AND PARENTING

There are many advantages to tranquility parenting, such as becoming calm, confident, and content as a parent. But to me, one of the most important benefits is having an integrated philosophy of both life and parenting. If I'm ever in a parenting quandary—should I buy the candy bar or not?—I don't need to refer to a list of rules about how to be a good parent. I don't need a degree in child psychology in order to figure out how to handle challenges. (Although that would probably help too.) Instead I can refer to the same principles that guide my decision making in the rest of my life. If Stoic philosophy guides my actions in other areas of life, why shouldn't it also guide my interactions with my children? If Stoic philosophy can teach me how to be truly happy and flourish, why can't it also teach my children how to be happy and flourish?

Before I adopted Stoicism as a philosophy of life, I was never sure if I was taking the right approach with my kids. If things didn't turn out the way I thought they should, I started doubting myself and my parenting abilities. Maybe I should have followed this parenting guide instead of that one? Maybe I used the wrong word or tone of voice? Maybe I was ruining my kids' chance of success in life?

I now realize that parenting doesn't come down to just one way of speaking or disciplining your kids. If you focus on just the superficial aspects without having an underlying philosophy, your approach is, so to speak, rootless. You don't have any firm convictions, and your methods are not anchored on anything solid. You may end up bouncing between different ideas or not really knowing why you are doing something. You could follow this suggestion or that one, with little real basis for choosing between them.

In tranquility parenting, our priorities are rooted in ancient wisdom. Our relationships with other people, our approach to overcoming challenges, our goals for our children, and the lessons we teach them are all based on Stoic philosophy. Our methods are rooted in our beliefs about what is important in life. When you focus on thinking clearly, acting wisely, and dealing with indifferents, you are not only becoming a better parent, you are also becoming a better person. And you are showing your child how to become a better person too.

Once you are confident in your priorities and what you should be teaching your child, you can use any strategies that work. Many discipline approaches are compatible with tranquility parenting, and there are many great ideas out there that can help us teach our children. The techniques we've discussed in this book are primarily designed to help you become calm, mindful, and engaged as a parent. Once you are in the right frame of mind, and you know what direction you want to move in, there are many different tactics you can use to guide your child.

I have just one recommendation as you scour books and websites for tactical advice: Keep your parenting philosophy firmly in your mind. There is so much information and so many opinions out there, and people tend to make us feel that we are doing things wrong. We start focusing on every little thing our child does, and we start feeling guilty, worried, anxious. . . . We don't want to go back in that direction, do we? I personally think we should focus on getting the big things right, things like truly appreciating our children and teaching them to be happy with what they have. The day-to-day parenting strategies we use with our kids should support those big goals, not the other way around. So as you search for advice on dealing with tricky childhood issues, be sure it fits into your overall priorities as a parent.

Remember, no matter how great a parent you are, you still cannot control how things turn out. Since we don't control the outcome of our actions, we should simply focus on doing the best we can. If your goal is to give your child a perfect life, you are guaranteed to be sorely disappointed. But if your goal is to help your child find *eudaimonia*, you can teach your child to flourish without having a perfect life. Maybe, despite your best efforts, things don't go perfectly. That's OK—you and your child can still be happy. And you know, your child will probably find happiness more easily if he doesn't expect life to be perfect. The road to happiness is paved with challenges. The important thing is having the wisdom to overcome them.

CHAPTER TAKEAWAYS

- Love plays a central role in everything you do as a parent. The more you learn to be calm, mindful, and engaged, the greater your capacity to love your child. By eliminating your negative emotions, you free up more energy to sincerely love and appreciate her.
- There are some emotions we should actually cultivate: enjoyment, cheerfulness, good spirits, goodwill, cherishing, and selfless love.
- There are two important ways we can show our love for our children: being virtuous and teaching them virtue. Even if we aren't perfect ourselves, we can still help our children find the path to flourishing.
- If you are fortunate enough to achieve *eudaimonia*, you will feel constantly joyful and cheerful. Your happiness will not depend on what anyone else does or what happens to you. Your joy will be strong and invincible.
- Many discipline approaches are compatible with tranquility parenting, and there are many great ideas out there that can help us teach our children. The techniques we've discussed in this book are primarily designed to help you become calm, mindful, and engaged as a parent. Once you are in the right frame of mind and know what

direction you want to move in, there are many different tactics you can use to guide your child.

- Your child will probably find happiness more easily if he doesn't expect a perfect life. The road to happiness is paved with challenges. The important thing is having the wisdom to overcome them.

MAKE IT YOUR OWN

As you work toward virtue for yourself and your child, think about the following parable from Epictetus:

> Nothing great comes into being all at once, for that is not the case even with a bunch of grapes or a fig. If you tell me now, "I want a fig," I'll reply, "That takes time." Let the fig tree first come into blossom and then bring forth its fruit, and then let the fruit grow to ripeness. So if even the fruit of a fig tree doesn't come to maturity all at once and in a single hour, would you seek to gather the fruit of a human mind in such a short time and with such ease?[10]

His point is that cultivating virtue is a slow process that can't be rushed. It takes constant care and nourishment. Only after you have patiently cultivated new mental habits will you see the fruits of your labor. Try to be patient with yourself and your child. Figs and grapes aren't produced in a day, and neither is wisdom or happiness. Learning virtue takes time.

II

Reference Section

9

PRACTICING TRANQUILITY

This chapter pulls together some of the core concepts and practical exercises I have recommended throughout the book. The purpose of including them again here is for you to be able to flip to the back of the book and quickly find what you need. Sometimes, when you're having a rough day, or even just a rough moment, it's helpful to refresh your memory with some Stoic pointers for tranquility.

You could also use these reminders as a sort of tranquility boot camp: Read through one each day and try to put it into practice. Or just write down some of your favorites on note cards or in your phone and look at them as often as you can. Try to keep these ideas fresh in your mind so that you have them ready during those difficult times when you need them. Don't be mad at yourself if you don't become a paragon of tranquility overnight. These things take time and practice to start working. Remember, you're rewiring your brain! This is not an easy thing to do. Just keep trying and eventually it will start to work for you.

DEFINING YOUR CORE BELIEFS

Everyday decision making is much easier if you already know what your core beliefs are. If you take time to think about your priorities before the need arises, you can quickly and efficiently handle challenges with your child. This helps reduce decision fatigue and ensures that you are consistent as a person and as a parent. You might choose to adopt Stoic principles as your core beliefs, or you might decide on something else. The important thing is that you know your core beliefs and then act on them.

DEALING WITH EMOTIONS

Our emotions result from our beliefs about what is right and wrong, good and bad, important and unimportant. For example, if you believe someone has harmed you, you will get angry. But if you don't think anyone is harming you, you have no reason to get angry. Stoic philosophy teaches us to remove our false beliefs that other people or situations are "bad." This helps us eliminate all negative emotions (anger, frustration, fear, anxiety, envy) and create space for positive emotions (joy, goodwill, cheerfulness). If your child misbehaves and you see it as a bad situation, you will feel frustrated. But if you recognize that it's just a normal situation that happens sometimes, you can stay calm and think clearly.

AIMING FOR VIRTUE

In Stoicism, virtue means excellence of mind and spirit. It consists of four main parts: wisdom, justice, courage, and self-control. If you manage to become completely virtuous, you understand everything you need to know about life, and as a result you become completely happy and fulfilled. Stoic philosophers say that virtue is necessary and sufficient for happiness. In other words, you must have virtue in order to be happy, and virtue is all you need to be happy. Therefore we want to become virtuous ourselves, and we want to help our children become virtuous. Stoicism is full of practical techniques on how to aim for virtue.

DEALING WITH INDIFFERENTS

Everything in life that is not morally good or bad is considered indifferent (money, social status, temper tantrums). These external things are not good or bad in themselves, but they can be used in good or bad ways. Some things are nice to have (financial security, good health, cooperative children); these are called preferred indifferents. It's fine for us to pursue these things as long as we do it wisely. We also want to teach our children that external things are never as important as being a good person.

TRANQUILITY PARENTING PHILOSOPHY

Our parenting philosophy should reflect our life philosophy. Tranquility parenting has three parts that should govern all our thoughts and actions: thinking clearly, acting wisely, and dealing with indifferents. Whenever you deal with a challenge, apply these steps and think about what is really important in the situation.

SOME THINGS ARE UP TO YOU, AND SOME THINGS ARE NOT

This is the most important concept in tranquility parenting. Some things are completely within your control, some things are completely outside your control, and some things you can influence but not control. Your child falls into this last category (influence but not control). If you try to control her, you will be unhappy and will never succeed. Instead, focus on those aspects of the situation you can control, including your own outlook, thought processes, and actions. Two specific techniques for this are internalizing your goals and focusing on input rather than outcome.

INTERNALIZING YOUR GOALS

In any situation, you can change your goal from something outside your control (*making* your child do his homework) to something within your control (*encouraging* your child to do his homework). This way, you always accomplish your goal of being a good parent, regardless of how your child responds. You will still have external strategies that you use to instruct, encourage, guide, and discipline. But your goal will be doing your best rather than forcing your child to do something.

FOCUSING ON INPUT RATHER THAN OUTCOME

You can control what you put into a situation, but you cannot control what results from it. So focus on what you put in: opinion, motivation, desires, aversions, and actions. Make your attitude and motivation the best they can be, and try to use the most effective strategies you can. Parents are like archers trying to hit a moving target: We can only do our best to aim; we cannot control whether we actually hit the target. We may not win every game, but we can still play the game well.

REMOVING NEGATIVE VALUE JUDGMENTS

We all form impressions about things around us. Stoics believe there are three parts to the subconscious process of forming an impression: perception, interpretation, and value judgment. The first two parts are relatively objective and neutral, but the third part (value judgment) is simply our opinion of how events relate to our lives. If we judge something to be good or bad when it is really indifferent, our value judgment is inaccurate. For example, a whiny child does not impact your personal virtue, so the situation is *indifferent* rather than *bad*. However, if you let yourself get frustrated and start yelling, your personal virtue is negatively impacted. Virtue only applies to things in your direct control, such as your own thoughts and behavior.

In order to bring our impressions of the world more in line with reality, we should eliminate untrue value judgments. Instead of thinking that something is bad for us, we should focus on what is within our control. So replace the value judgment with your decision and reaction. Try to judge the situation objectively and remember that cranky kids and difficult days are just indifferents. That way, you can stop wasting your mental energy, since you realize there is nothing to get upset about in the first place.

PHYSICAL DEFINITION

Break down your challenges into their component parts or materials. A temper tantrum is nothing more than a frustrated child crying and stomping. Seeing it this way helps us keep the situation in perspective—it's not the end of the world; it's just a series of small, everyday events. You can handle it more easily and calmly if you think about it in terms of smaller parts. There is always more than one way to look at a situation!

THE INNER CITADEL

Once you learn to apply accurate judgment to everything around you, your good judgment becomes an inner refuge, or place of strength. No matter what difficulties arise, you can decide not to let them upset you. It takes a lot of practice to consistently remove false value judgments from your impressions. But if you can understand and control your own thought processes, you are in a position of inner peace, strength, and contentment.

NO ONE MAKES MISTAKES INTENTIONALLY

Your child is not trying to be bad—she just hasn't learned the right way to behave. That means she needs your guidance and correction. Instead of seeing misbehavior as a desire to make you mad, try not to take it personally. If you take misbehavior as a personal insult, you will get angry and discipline out of anger. Instead, see it as an opportunity for you to show your child how to stay calm and handle challenges in a constructive way.

CHANGING YOUR CHILD'S CALCULATION OF INTEREST

People act in ways they think will benefit them. If your child misbehaves, it's because he thinks whatever he is doing is in his own best interest. To correct his misbehavior, you have to show him that it's really not in his best interest. You can do this through positive or negative reinforcement, persuasion, or whatever you think will work. The preferred method is explaining your moral reasoning. This way your child learns that all your decisions are guided by an ethical code. The sooner you start talking to your child about moral reasoning, the sooner he will understand and accept it.

EXPECTING TO DEAL WITH PROBLEMS

From the time you get up in the morning, expect that your child will challenge you and need your guidance. In your morning reflection, think about what issues you might face that day. Try to think of two or three ways you can respond constructively, and maybe even visualize yourself calmly dealing with the problem. That way, when the challenge actually happens, you will be prepared. But remember, you can't plan for everything, so also expect the unexpected! If you expect to deal with problems, you will never be disappointed.

BEING KIND AND BENEVOLENT

You are your child's teacher, and sometimes you need to be firm and set boundaries. But you can still do this with peace and kindness. There is a difference between being kind and being lax, and there is a difference between firmness and harshness. Our goal is to be wise, kind, loving, and firm when necessary. When your child misbehaves, it means he needs your guidance. Be a role model and show him how to approach frustrations with patience and dignity. If you don't show him this, who will?

DEALING WITH OTHER PEOPLE'S OPINIONS

Everyone loves to tell parents how to raise their kids. It can be frustrating and upsetting when other people criticize your parenting style. Here are my suggestions:

1. **Remember that the criticizer is misguided.** She probably thinks she is helping, even if in reality she is doing the opposite. She wants her opinion to matter.
2. **You can choose not to be offended.** Just because someone criticizes you doesn't mean you have to get upset. Just see the criticism for what it is: a reflection of the criticizer's flaws, not your own.
3. **Think about the source of the criticism.** If it's someone who truly has your child's best interests at heart, acknowledge her good intentions. Think about whether you should accept the advice. If it's someone not relevant to your child at all, feel free to ignore or deflect the unwanted advice.
4. **Remember that criticism is a dispreferred indifferent.** It doesn't impact your happiness unless you let it. If you respond wisely, you are no worse off. But if you respond with anger, you have injured yourself.
5. **Expect to deal with criticism.** It happens to everyone, not just you. Think in advance about how you might handle criticism from different sources.
6. **Don't be a criticizer yourself.** Try not to judge people without knowing their reasons and intentions. Remember to treat others the way you want them to treat you.

TALKING ABOUT VIRTUE

Children are born with a basic affinity for other people, but they don't always know how to behave well. We should give them the vocabulary and concepts to start talking about ethics from a young age. As you go through your day, talk to your kids about your own ethical decision making and your expectations for their behavior. You could explain to them that you don't always enjoy doing some things (like cleaning up) but that you do it anyway because the house needs to stay clean. In the same way, you expect them to clean up after themselves because it's part of living together as a family. They may not always understand what you mean, but they will start to understand that your behavior is guided by an ethical system. With enough practice, they will also understand that their own behavior should be guided by ethical considerations.

TEACHING VIRTUE

You can teach a kid-friendly version of Stoic philosophy to help guide your child's behavior. The three parts match up to our tranquility parenting philosophy:

1. You control yourself, not other people.
2. Treat other people the way you want them to treat you.
3. Don't get upset, just deal with the problem.

It's easy to find teachable moments throughout the day to instruct your child in these core concepts. Try to reach your child on her level and develop concrete metaphors or ways of talking about these principles. When she runs into problems or frustrations, you can help her find a solution using one of the three core concepts.

1. **You control yourself, not other people.** This is the kid-friendly version of *thinking clearly*, and it is one of the hardest concepts to learn. Teach her to calm herself down when she is angry, and to focus on her own behavior rather than worrying about someone else's. The overall goal is to help her learn to think about her own thoughts and actions.
2. **Treat other people the way you want them to treat you.** This is the kid-friendly version of *acting wisely*. You are helping your child learn good behavior by thinking about other people's feelings. We do this by helping others, being kind to friends and siblings, and noticing how good it feels to be good.
3. **Don't get upset, just deal with the problem.** This is the kid-friendly version of *dealing with indifferents*. Your basic goal in teaching this principle is to help your child develop self-control and emotional awareness. Some of the skills to work on are being patient and dealing with frustration, fear, and discomfort.

LIVING IN THE HERE AND NOW

Learn to focus your attention not on what you're doing tomorrow and not on what you didn't get done yesterday. Focus on just you and your child, right at this moment. What is your child doing? What does she need from you right now? What wonderful thing do you love about her right now? You don't want to look back when your child is grown and realize that you weren't fully present while she was growing up. There's no need to feel guilty about what you can't give your child. Just give her what you can, but be completely there when you are with her.

IT'S NOT AS BAD AS YOU THINK (PROJECTIVE VISUALIZATION)

Imagine someone else is going through the same thing you are. What would you advise that parent to do? Would you advise him to get frustrated and upset with his child? Or would you advise him to rethink his value judgments and remember that this is not worth getting upset about? It's easier to be objective when something happens to someone else. Now, apply that same advice to yourself. Try to handle the situation as though a wise person is looking over your shoulder.

WANTING WHAT YOU HAVE (NEGATIVE VISUALIZATION)

If you expect a perfect child or a problem-free life, you will always be disappointed. But if you make a conscious decision to be content with what you have, you can be thankful for your imperfect but lovable child (instead of wanting an imaginary ideal). What if you didn't have your child at all? Our children give us joy and love. Instead of wanting the impossible, be happy with what you have.

KEEPING THINGS IN PERSPECTIVE

Zoom out for a moment and think about all the millions of children and parents all over the world. Don't you think those children are testing their parents' patience too? Don't you think the other parents have just as much to deal with as you do? It might sometimes seem like everyone else has things easier than you do, but that's a false impression. All parents have to deal with frustrations. You just don't usually get a chance to see what happens in other people's lives.

REFLECTION (MORNING AND EVENING)

Take sixty seconds in the morning and evening to think about your parenting practices. Try to make it a part of your routine that you can't skip. In the morning, think about what challenges you might face with your child that day. Brainstorm a few solutions that align with your core beliefs and parenting philosophy. Later in the day, when that challenging situation arises, you will already have a good solution up your sleeve.

In the evening, reflect on how you handled any challenges that actually arose. Did you remember to think clearly, act wisely, and deal with indifferents? If you didn't, don't get mad at yourself; just think about how you can improve tomorrow. If you made progress that day, be proud of your small victory and do it again the next day.

REPAIRING YOUR VALUE JUDGMENTS

Just as you can rethink your value judgments as you make everyday decisions, you can repair the value judgments that lead to fear and anxiety. Remember the three parts of every impression: perception, interpretation, and value judgment. The perception and impression are neutral, but the value judgment is just an opinion you add at the end. Work on eliminating the inaccurate opinion that something bad is about to happen to your child. Replace the false value judgment with a neutral decision and reaction.

If your child is sick, don't add, "He's going to have life-threatening complications," in your head. Eliminate the value judgment and focus on your decision ("I need to stay calm and call the doctor") and reaction (call the doctor, keep your child comfortable, stay calm). You can keep an eye out for anything worrisome but not actually worry about it. Worrying does not help anything, and it stresses your child and clouds your judgment. Staying calm and rational does help and is always the preferred mode for handling emergencies.

FINDING A COURAGEOUS ROLE MODEL

If you find yourself worrying about your child, try to find a courageous role model you can think of when anxiety starts creeping up on you. It could be a real or fictional person. Think about how that person would react if he or she faced the same situation you are facing. In the face of hardship or danger, what would that person think? What would he or she do? Try to do whatever that person would do in your situation.

BEING A COURAGEOUS ROLE MODEL

When your child grows up and looks back on his childhood, how do you want him to remember you? As anxious and overprotective, or as wise and courageous? Be a role model for your child. Imagine that one day he is facing the same difficult situation you are facing right now. Would you advise him to fret and worry, or to stay calm and focus on what he can control? He is 100 percent guaranteed to experience some problems in life, and he will probably think back to how he saw you handling problems. Be sure you set a courageous example.

USING YOUR MANTRA

In tranquility parenting, you don't need to shut your brain off—you just need to turn bad thoughts into goods ones. It's OK if you can't clear your mind. You can keep thinking, but be sure you are thinking clearly and using good judgment. It's up to you to decide which thoughts are allowed in your brain. If you usually worry, start training your brain to go down a different path. Have a mantra ready to use, and pull it out whenever your thoughts go in the wrong direction. Changing your mental habits is a difficult process, so be patient and reward yourself for small victories.

THE GOOD EMOTIONS

Remember, Stoicism is not about eliminating all emotion; it's about eliminating bad emotions. That leaves more room for positive emotions such as joy, cheerfulness, and goodwill. Once you train yourself to make good judgments and focus on what you can control, you will feel a constant contentment and cheerfulness. This is why we want to aim for virtue, and it's why we want to show our children how to find virtue and happiness.

10

DEALING WITH DIFFICULT SITUATIONS

Throughout this book we've talked about many concepts and strategies for staying calm while you deal with difficult situations. In this chapter, I will make specific suggestions for dealing with several classic challenges. Keep in mind that these are only suggestions and may not apply to your particular circumstances. Every family and every child is unique. Feel free to adapt these suggestions as necessary. There is no way anyone else can know what is best for you and your child, so be sure to use your judgment as to what will work. You might also want to try several different approaches to see what works best.

Most of all, please do not think there's anything wrong with you or your child just because you are different from other people. Different things work for different families. There isn't just one right way to raise your child. Just remember to use your good judgment and internalize your goals while you are working through these issues. And remember the end point of all our efforts: to find contentment and tranquility and to help our children flourish. That's what it's all about, right?

These ten scenarios are arranged by age group, with youngest children first and oldest children last. With a few adaptations, some of the scenarios in the middle can apply to children of all ages.

TANTRUMMING

- **Stay tranquil.** The first person to work on in this situation is your-self. Before you can deal with your child, you have to deal with your own negative emotions. Are you embarrassed, irritated, or discouraged? Stay strong in your inner citadel. Remember that this situation is merely a dispreferred indifferent, not something morally bad. You've done nothing wrong, and you have nothing to be ashamed of. Remove your false value judgment and replace it with a rational decision and reaction.
- **Speak calmly.** When you're in control of your judgment, speak calmly to your child. This may not have an immediate effect if your child is really in a rage, but it's worth a try. If you're in the habit of talking about ethics with your child, she will be used to having this kind of conversation with you. Try to build up this habit in calmer moments so that you can rely on it in times of crisis.
- **Empathize and redirect.** Tell your child that you know she's frustrated but that kicking and screaming is not the right way to deal with her frustration. Suggest some alternative physical expressions of frustration: stamping her feet, jumping up and down, making a silly face, or making funny noises—whatever works for both of you.
- **Give a hug if your child wants one.** Sometimes kids want a hug, and sometimes it just makes them even madder. If she doesn't want a hug, try another physical connection, like patting her back or holding her hand.
- **Use humor if you can.** Once the edge is off your child's frustration, you can help her calm down completely. If I have a mirror in my purse, I take it out and show my kids how their faces look when they're angry. This usually makes them laugh and calm down. Or you can try your own silly faces or jokes to get your child's mind off her anger.
- **Teach techniques for self-calming.** Try the classics: taking a deep breath, counting to five (or however high your child can count), repeating a soothing phrase to herself. These might be more or less effective depending on your child's age and personality.
- **Address the source of the frustration.** Once your child is calm, you can talk about why she couldn't have the candy or toy. This is the core of the situation. If you don't address the underlying cause, the

tantrum is likely to happen again when she doesn't get what she wants. Once your child understands that she doesn't get everything she wants, she will stop throwing tantrums.

- **Teach self-control in daily life.** Build this into your everyday interactions with your child. No matter how young she is, you can start teaching that she can't have everything she wants. Be sure to do it gently and kindly. Teaching self-control doesn't require you to be mean or severe. Stay calm by focusing on what you can control and by replacing false value judgments with a rational decision and reaction. This is a very hard lesson for kids to learn; it takes time and lots of guidance from you.

POTTY TRAINING

- **Believe it or not, this phase will pass.** Potty training is one of the few behavior challenges that should resolve on its own as your child gets older. At some point your child will learn to use the potty by himself. The big question is how to stay sane until you get there.
- **Stay positive** (positive reinforcement). Since you know your child will eventually learn to use the potty, there's no need to turn this into a negative situation. Threats and negative reinforcement will probably not toilet train your child. So why make the situation more difficult than it already is? Make things as fun as possible; use encouragement and rewards if you need to.
- **Wait until your child is ready.** Potty training is both physical and psychological. Even if you know your child is capable of controlling his physical functions, he may not understand why he needs to. If you try to force your child to train before he is ready, you will both be miserable.
- **Manage your expectations.** Don't expect your child to train in a week, and try not to compare his progress with all the other preschoolers you know. That will just make you feel bad about yourself and your child. Remember that there is a range of normal behavior, which your pediatrician can help you identify. Expect to have challenges (and messes). Be proactive and think about how to encourage your child through this once-in-a-lifetime experience.

- **Focus on what you can control.** You can't force your child to potty train. If you feel yourself getting frustrated with a lack of progress, go back to the trichotomy of control: Internalize your goals, focus on your own input, and remember that this is not a "bad" situation. And keep things in perspective: Children have learned these skills since the beginning of time. Yours will learn too . . . eventually.

NOT FOLLOWING DIRECTIONS

- **Don't take it personally.** Your child is not misbehaving because he wants to be bad. He just hasn't learned the right way to behave. That means he needs your guidance, not your anger. See this as an opportunity for teaching him how to be a good person.
- **Understand your child's motivation.** Your child thinks he's acting in his best interest. To correct his misbehavior, show him that following your directions is actually in his best interest. First step: Reason with him. Relate your expectations back to your code of ethics. "My responsibility is to take care of you, and your responsibility is to follow my directions. That's how we care for one another in our family. I have to teach you the right way to do things."
- **Try a different approach.** If he's too young or your reasoning doesn't work, try other strategies: jokes, reminders, positive or negative reinforcement, etc. Don't get frustrated. If something doesn't work one time, try something else the next time.
- **Try to plan ahead** (premeditation of adversity). If he consistently doesn't follow directions, try to do some preparation so that you are ready for his challenges. In those moments when he *is* minding well, praise and encourage him. Talk about your expectations and how important it is for him to do what you ask. If you only pull out the moral reasoning when he's misbehaving, he will think of it as a punishment. Talk about your moral reasoning all the time so that he knows it guides everything you do.

FIGHTING WITH A SIBLING (YOUNGER KIDS)

- **Understand human nature.** Humans are born with an instinct for self-preservation. A big part of growing up is learning that other people's needs matter just as much as yours do. However, this is a slow and difficult lesson to learn, so we have to be patient as we encourage our kids to think about other people. As the parent, we can see that baby brother didn't mean to mess up his big sister's block city. But to a three- or four-year-old, it seems like the baby intentionally ruined her life. She feels perfectly justified in taking the law into her own hands.
- **Defuse the situation by showing that you understand why she's upset.** "You worked really hard on your block city, and it looked great! I can understand why you're mad at your brother."
- **Then try to show her she can deal with her frustration in a positive way.** "You know, just because you feel frustrated doesn't mean you should hit Freddy. He's a baby—do you think he meant to hurt your city? He thought it was really cool and wanted to play with you. Babies just don't know how to play the way you do."
- **Help your child understand that instead of getting upset, she can fix the problem.** "Now you get to build your city again! That's the fun part. I'll keep Freddy away while you rebuild."
- **In a way, you are helping your child adopt a Stoic outlook on problem-solving:** eliminating negative emotions by making correct judgments about what is important. Just like it helps us as adults, it can also help children work through their problems. You can start to teach your child that some things in life are not worth getting upset about.

DEALING WITH FRUSTRATION

- **Dealing with frustration is a vital life skill.** Think of all the frustrations, big and small, you have encountered in your own life. As you're helping your child cope with frustration, remember that your coaching can help him become calmer and more patient for the rest of his life. Don't just think he will grow out of his frustrations. Help him deal with them head-on.

- **What works for you could work for them too.** Many of the techniques we have discussed for parents can also help children handle negative emotions. Our basic parenting philosophy says it all: Think clearly, act wisely, and deal with indifferents. If you can teach your child how to do these three things, he will be capable of working through difficult situations for the rest of his life.
- **Start with *thinking clearly*.** Let's say your child is having trouble getting his shoes on by himself. He might whine, throw his shoe down, and refuse to try again. Use this as an opportunity to teach him to think clearly about the situation. Some kids feel overwhelmed by their emotions and give up easily. Help him work through the emotion and look at the situation differently. "I know you're frustrated, but is this something to get upset about?" Try to make it concrete and reach him on his level. For example, "Are you about to fall in a volcano? Are you about to get eaten by a dinosaur? No!" Some kid humor can help him understand that this particular frustration is not the end of the world, so he doesn't need to get upset. This is part of developing good judgment about what matters in life and what is within his control. Why not start teaching him good judgment now?
- **Don't just tell him to be patient.** Explain why and how he should be patient. You've already explained that this is just a small problem, not worth getting upset about. You can also tell him, "You can solve problems better if you're not upset. Your brain can't think about two things at once. If your brain is thinking about being mad, it can't think about putting your shoes on." Use his role models: "Does [insert superhero here] get upset and start crying?" Even bigger kids that he knows can be role models. Just like we use role models for ourselves as adults, children can have role models too!
- **Move on to the solution.** After you've both decided this is not a serious issue, move on to solving the problem. If your child is calm and not frustrated anymore, he should be able to try again; but if he hasn't gotten the thinking clearly part first, it will be difficult for him to stay patient and keep trying. This is where patience and perseverance come in. Help your child think about solving the problem step by step. Can you break it down for him and explain it on his level?
- **Don't be afraid to help.** It's OK to do things for your child if he's just not developmentally ready. If you think he is truly able to put his shoes on and is just being lazy, then you might want to make him try

harder. But if he's really trying and still can't do it, you can tell him that there's nothing wrong with getting a little help. Everyone needs help sometimes. He can practice more tomorrow and he'll get it soon.

COMPETITION/JEALOUSY

- **Competition between siblings is natural.** Parents have a finite amount of attention and resources, and each child wants 100 percent. What can you do to minimize competition? The first step is to actively develop an environment of camaraderie and affection at home. Praise your children for being kind to each other. Teach them to praise each other.
- **You're all on the same team.** I like to use a team metaphor for our family. My older two children are very outgoing and have always competed for attention. I have to remind them that we are all on the same team—when one person wins, we all win. When one person loses, we all lose. We feel happy for one another, we love one another, we help one another. We share what we have, and we enjoy spending time together. If you repeat it often enough—and reinforce caring behaviors—your kids will start to believe it.
- **Set up clear rules for sharing.** Then when a specific situation arises, you can remind your kids of the family rules. In our house, we have a rule that our kids can play with their toys in their own room as much as they want. But if they bring a toy into the family room, they have to let their siblings have a turn with it. This very clear rule helps defuse arguments because we know what the solution is (take the toy into your room).
- **Help your kids become active participants in finding a solution.** Talk about the situation. "I know you both want my attention, but I can't give it to you at the same time. What should we do about this?" Sometimes they will surprise you with reasonable suggestions. See if you can incorporate their input, but even if you don't, be positive toward their suggestions. This approach has several benefits:

1. It helps your children see the situation itself, not the other sibling, as problematic. This removes the sting of personal insult for your kids and helps everyone stay calm.
2. It sends the message that the problem is solvable, and that you can solve it together as a family. Working through problems as a team will encourage your kids to build trust with each other.
3. It helps build general problem-solving skills. Once your children learn to get along with each other, they can apply the same skills to getting along with other people. And we all know what a valuable skill that is!

- **Expect your children to get along.** Your expectations are important. After all, it's unlikely your kids will make an effort to get along if you don't reinforce it. The easy route, or default mode, is to just deal with each fight as it comes along. But remember, we don't want to slide by in default mode. We want to be principled in dealing with problems. If you actively foster an atmosphere of warmth and mutual care, your kids will pick up on it and (eventually) start to do it themselves.

FIGHTING WITH A SIBLING (OLDER KIDS)

- **Do some reconnaissance to get the whole story.** When a fight breaks out, it's rare that only one person is completely at fault. Most of the time, it takes two to tango.
- **Talk to both children about their actions.** Maybe one of them lashed out, but the other one provoked. Assign consequences for both of them (not necessarily the same consequences, but enough so that they both understand they are at fault). Consequences don't have to be some form of punishment, but they should involve a recognition on the child's part that he has not acted wisely.
- **Connect your actions and your children's actions to your code of ethics.** You don't enjoy lecturing or disciplining them, but it's your responsibility to teach them the right way to behave. Therefore you have to correct them, whether you want to or not.
- **Help them link their actions to their own ethical understanding.** Do they feel proud of themselves? Were they kind? Would they

want someone to act that way toward them? The goal is for your child to be his own conscience so that you don't have to be.

- **Remind your kids that you are all on the same team.** When one person wins, you all win. Try to build a sense of family camaraderie rather than of competition. Practice being happy for one another's successes, praising one another, and doing kind things for one another. The more practice your kids have with kind actions, the more likely they are to default to kindness.

PROBLEMS WITH OTHER CHILDREN AT SCHOOL

- **Advising your child on how to deal with other people is tough.** Your first impulse may be to go deal with the problem yourself. Sometimes this is the right thing to do, as in cases of bullying or other abuse. However, for less serious issues, it may be better to help your child help himself. The reason is simple: You will be teaching your child how to handle problems in life. Even as an adult, your child is sure to run into problematic people and situations. You want him to be equipped to handle these. Letting him practice is the best way for him to learn these skills. It's up to your good judgment to decide when you should get involved and when you should teach your child to solve his own problems.
- **Other people don't always behave well.** If your child is being teased or excluded, he has already started learning some of the hard lessons about how other people behave. Don't you wish you could tell him that adults behave better than teenagers? Sadly, many adults do not act wisely either, so the lessons he learns now can help him for the rest of his life. Many of the strategies we discussed in chapter 4 will be useful for your child in dealing with his classmates.
- **Ignore them if you can.** There are two basic strategies for dealing with unpleasant people: Ignore or engage. These might be appropriate in different situations, so again, you'll have to think through which is the best option for this situation. If you advise your child to ignore his mean classmates, be sure he understands the theory behind your advice. Those people are ignorant of the right way to be happy, and they have chosen the wrong way to behave. Their taunts are a reflection of their own shortcomings, not your son's. There will

always be ignorant and malicious people in the world, so don't let them get to you. Encourage your son to focus on his own gifts in life: friends, studies, hobbies, family, his future, etc.

- **But if you can't ignore them . . .** Alternatively, if you advise your son to engage with the mean schoolmates, there are different strategies for standing up to them or deflecting their taunts. One is to laugh them off. Epictetus used to tell people who insulted him that they were wrong to criticize so little about him—he was actually much worse than they imagined! Another is to directly confront their vicious tactics. However, telling off an antagonistic classmate may not change his behavior—he may even try to retaliate. If necessary, you can escalate the issue to the responsible adult.
- **You're better than that.** Through it all, remind your son that just because other people act badly, it doesn't impact his own character. Throughout history there have been bullies and malicious people who tried to enrich themselves and harm others. There will always be such people in the world. But at the same time, there have always been wise and brave people who stood up to them. You can give historical examples like Socrates and William Wallace (of *Braveheart* fame) and find many books and movies with similar themes (*Star Wars, Harry Potter*). Perhaps your son will take heart from famous heroes who have lived through similar experiences and prospered.
- **Teach your child to work toward a better world, but to accept the limitations of what he can do.** Yes, we should stand up for ourselves and try to improve the world. But we have to remember that it is beyond our power to change the way other people behave. At most we can influence them. Help your son learn this crucial distinction. We do what we can, and we have to let the rest go.
- **Help your child build a firm foundation of confidence in his inner character.** Try to emphasize that we can still be happy no matter what other people do to us. The only thing we need to be happy is to strive for personal excellence, regardless of what happens around us. This is an excellent opportunity to help your child find the path to flourishing—not by seeking approval from other people but by seeking approval from himself.

NOT DOING HOMEWORK

- **Do not start a power struggle.** If you command your child to do something "because I said so," that opens the door to a long battle over your authority. Remember, don't take your child's behavior personally. You already know you're right because you've thought about the issue carefully and applied your philosophy of life. You don't have to prove to your child that you're right. Keep your own ego out of the situation.

- **Try to understand why your child is refusing to do homework.** There could be many issues going on under the surface: She doesn't like the subject or is struggling to keep up; the teacher embarrassed her in class; her friends don't think it's cool to do homework; she's just more interested in other aspects of life right now. If you can diagnose the root cause of the problem, you will be better at helping to fix it.

- **Talk calmly with your child.** You don't need to be buddy-buddy with her, but if you talk to her as one rational person to another, you might both be able to uncover the problem. She herself might not be fully aware of her motivations; talking through it with you could help her understand herself.

- **Frame your concern in terms of your child's well-being.** This is not about you; it's about her. Let her know that you want to help her flourish. Try to stay away from phrases like "You're ruining your future," or "You'll never go to college." Those distant concerns are probably not going to sway your child at a moment like this. Also try not to accuse and blame ("I can't believe you're doing this!" "How could you fail a test?"). That is not going to help anything, and it will probably just make thing worse. Instead, approach the problem from your concern about your child's well-being. Not doing homework is a sign that she is not making good judgments about the world.

- **Make your expectations clear.** Explain that you expect her to do her homework without a fuss, and explain your reasons.

- **Figure out what motivates your child.** You can try everything in your power to force her to do homework, but if she's made up her mind not to do it, she won't. Your best strategy is to change her calculation of what's in her interest. If you can convince her that doing homework is in her best interest, she will do it. So think about what makes your daughter tick. Is she a social butterfly? Is she a bookworm? Does she want to be a chef, a pro tennis player, or a biologist? If you know what she loves, you can relate it back to why she should do her homework. As the adult, you have the life experience to know that doing her homework is ultimately going to make her life better. But she may not be able to see that unless you show her. Keep in mind that every child is different, so what works for some children may not work for others. If you have two or more children, chances are they will each be motivated by different things.

- **Try not to bargain.** You don't control your child, but you do have all the authority in the situation. Your child might try something like "I'll do my homework if you buy me a new tablet." Don't fall for it. If you allow her to bargain like this, you've set up a superficial transaction. You are sending the message that all you care about is getting the homework done rather than your daughter's character and ability to flourish. This might work in the short term, but in the long term she will expect you to keep giving her stuff in return for her cooperation. Bad outlook. Instead, make it clear that you expect her to do her homework because of the reasons you explained earlier. (Keep repeating them if necessary.) If your true concern is her character and ability to flourish, then getting the homework done is a secondary matter. Keep your focus on what really matters: your daughter's long-term well-being.

- **Focus on what is in your control.** When it comes down to it, you can't force your daughter to do something. Keep in mind the trichotomy of control throughout the whole interaction. Also remember to internalize your goals and focus on your own input into the situation. If you have given your best effort to reach your daughter and help her start doing homework, that's all you can do. That doesn't mean you should give up if it doesn't work on the first try. It means you should stay calm and think about a better approach. Changing her mind—and her behavior—might take time.

TALKING BACK

- **Choose not to be offended.** If you're on autopilot, you might take it personally when your child says something rude to you. But in tranquility parenting, we are never on autopilot. We focus on the big picture of parenting and remember to think clearly, act wisely, and deal with indifferents. Like many other challenges, this one is just a dispreferred indifferent. There's no need to get angry. In fact, if you get angry, you will almost certainly think fuzzily and act unwisely. To avoid getting angry, remove your false value judgment that something bad has happened to you.

- **Keep things in perspective.** You are not the only parent in the world who has to deal with a smart-alecky teenager. Don't feel like fate has conspired against you—this is something many parents have dealt with. The key is to find a calm and proactive way to deal with the issue.

- **Choose your response:** Ignore, deflect, or address your child's remark. If it's a one-time occurrence, maybe ignoring it is the best response. However, it's probably better to address it directly to prevent it from happening again. Humor can be a good strategy if you have the presence of mind to joke about the remark. You can always use the technique William Irvine recommends for joking away insults: "You don't know the half of it! If you only knew me better, you'd have a lot more to insult." Whichever response you choose, be sure you are genuinely not offended. Teenagers can easily tell if they're getting to you.

- **Remind your child that you are acting in the way you think is best for her.** But make sure this is actually true—if you are angry, you will not be acting in her best interest. Keep your mind clear so that you do not discipline out of anger. You want to teach her to be respectful to her parents because you're educating her about virtue, not because you feel disrespected.

- **If you are still upset, try to break down the situation into its component parts.** Your daughter merely uttered certain words to you. This is not the worst thing that has ever happened; she's just a kid trying to get her way by using normal teenage tactics. Yes, your teenager is probably trying to make you mad. Yes, she probably knows exactly which buttons to push. So remove the buttons. Be the bigger person—because that's what you are, right?

- **Emphasize your expectations for her participation in the family.** She is probably not going to like everything you want her to do, but she still needs to do it as a daughter and member of the family.

Everyone pitches in. Just like you have to do many things you don't like, so does she. So does everyone else in the world. It's just part of being a person. She can do them and be unhappy, or she can do them and be happy. You might want to remind her that she will have to do many more things in life that she doesn't want to do, so this is good practice.

- **Ask your daughter to think about the situation from your perspective.** If she had worked really hard to take care of someone and they said something rude and ungrateful, how would she feel?
- **Remind her that you are all on the same team and all want the same thing:** to be happy and live a meaningful life. Why should you waste time being rude to each other? It's a much better idea to figure out a way to get along so that you can spend time enjoying each other's company. If you're both respectful to each other, you can talk things out and move on. If one person refuses to be reasonable, that person is going to waste a lot of time being unhappy.

APPENDIX

Learning More About Stoicism

Congratulations—you made it to the end of the book! If you've stuck with it this far, you're already on your way to a deeper appreciation of Stoic principles and practices. But of course, this book focuses specifically on applying those principles to parenting, not on Stoicism itself. If you feel this approach is working for you and you'd like to learn more, there are many great resources out there. Below, I list my recommendations for anyone who wants to keep learning about this ancient wisdom tradition.

If you're already exhausted by everything we've talked about in *Tranquility Parenting*, don't feel like you have to read anything else. What we've covered already is enough for you to become a calm, mindful, and engaged parent. Just remember, Rome wasn't built in a day. Start small and keep trying. It's very hard to rewire your brain and change your thought processes, which is essentially what Stoicism asks you to do. But the payoff is worth it: tranquility, peace of mind, fulfillment, and contentment. So keep practicing, and keep going back to chapters 9 and 10 to refresh your memory. It might not work for you immediately, but it will work for you eventually. Stoicism is a time-tested tradition. It's still around today because it works.

If you are eager to read more, I suggest that you start with a few of the key books and websites in the Stoic community. Here are three great books that provide a general overview of Stoic philosophy:

- *A Guide to the Good Life: The Ancient Art of Stoic Joy* **(William Irvine).** Irvine's book was one of the first Stoic works to reach a wide audience in the twenty-first century. He starts from the very beginning and offers compelling reasons why we should adopt a Stoic outlook on life. He also provides short, readable chapters on complicated questions, like dealing with insults and overcoming anger.
- *How to Be a Stoic: Using Ancient Philosophy to Live a Modern Life* **(Massimo Pigliucci).** Pigliucci explains why we all need philosophy as a guide for life, and in particular why Stoic philosophy is a good choice. In the book, he takes inspiration from Epictetus and visits ancient sites like Rome and Istanbul. He also addresses potential questions and concerns about how Stoicism fits with current social issues.
- *Stoicism and the Art of Happiness* **(Donald Robertson).** Robertson is a psychotherapist who connects Stoic theory to contemporary psychotherapy techniques. His book provides excellent concrete advice for eliminating negative emotions and living a satisfying life. He also clearly explains the psychological basis for many ancient Stoic principles.

If you prefer to go straight to the original ancient sources, there are many translations from the Greek and Roman texts. Here are some very accessible versions:

- **Marcus Aurelius:** *Meditations* **(Robin Hard translation).** This collection of Marcus's private thoughts shows us how to put Stoic principles into practice. Some of his remarks can be a little cryptic, but you now have enough Stoic knowledge to understand most of his ideas. Short and inspiring, this is a great place to start with the ancient literature. (*Note:* There are many different translations available. Be sure to check which translation you are getting. Some are harder to read than others.)
- **Epictetus:** *Discourses, Fragments, Handbook* **(Robin Hard translation).** Epictetus tells it like it is. I really like this translation, which includes all the available lectures attributed to Epictetus. You might want to actually flip to the back and start with the *Handbook*, since it is more direct and accessible. If you are ready

for detailed explanations of Stoic principles, the *Discourses* are incredibly valuable. They make you wish you could have been a student in Epictetus's ancient classroom.

- **Seneca: *Selected Letters*.** Seneca's language is ornate and polished, but his advice is still logical and accessible in this collection of letters. Here Seneca advises a friend named Lucilius on how to deal with the troubles and temptations of life. The letters also offer a glimpse of upper-class ancient Roman life, which was not so very different from twenty-first-century Western society. This is one of my favorite reads for practical Stoic advice.

In addition, there are some very helpful websites that will help deepen your understanding of Stoic practice. New ones are being created all the time. Here are just a few:

- **Modern Stoicism (http://modernstoicism.com).** This is the flagship online resource for all things Stoic. Founded by a committed group of professors and psychotherapists, Modern Stoicism will keep you up to date with new events and ideas in the Stoic world. One of its most useful features is the *Stoicism Today* blog, which hosts articles on how a wide variety of people apply Stoicism in daily life. This is a great place to start if you want to learn more about the Stoic community and practices.
- **How to Be a Stoic (https://howtobeastoic.wordpress.com).** Massimo Pigliucci, author of the book *How to Be a Stoic*, also maintains an excellent blog on Stoic issues. He includes book reviews, in-depth analyses of difficult problems, comparisons of Stoicism with other philosophical practices, and a Stoic advice column. The site is interesting, useful, and accessible.
- **Donald Robertson's training courses (https://learn.donaldrobertson.name).** Robertson is the psychotherapist behind *Stoicism and the Art of Happiness* and one of the guiding spirits behind the modern Stoic movement. He offers many excellent resources on his website, including a "Crash Course in Stoicism," a "Stoic Therapy Toolkit," a course on "How to Think Like a Roman Emperor," as well as a newsletter and articles. This is the place to go if you would like information about

the therapeutic benefits of Stoicism or on connections between therapy and philosophy.

- **Gregory B. Sadler's YouTube channel (www.youtube.com/ user/gbisadler).** Greg Sadler shares his lectures and musings on philosophy with over 50,000 subscribers to this entertaining and instructional channel. While the channel contains videos on all kinds of philosophy, many are specifically on Stoic concepts and living. Sadler also offers philosophical counseling through his consultancy, ReasonIO.

I also recommend the following websites about philosophical parenting. The first two sites relate parenting to general philosophy, so you will learn how to apply a variety of philosophical principles to modern life.

- **Common Sense Ethics (www.commonsenseethics.com).** Leah Goldrick maintains a website devoted to "living a good life, becoming a better person, and exploring the human condition." She offers interesting resources and articles for connecting philosophy to everyday ethical living. Topics include ethics in popular culture, dealing with the news media, knowing yourself better, and creating your ideal family culture.
- **Philosophy for Parents (https://philosophyforparents.com).** This site by Holly Hamilton-Bleakley covers a wide range of philosophical topics, including "Cartesian-Inspired Thoughts on the Value of Caregiving," anger management recommendations by Plato, how to deal with summer vacations, and more.
- **Apparent Stoic (www.apparentstoic.com).** This is my own website on Stoic parenting, which builds on many of the principles I introduced in this book. Now that you have background knowledge of Stoicism, you might be interested in exploring some of these ideas in more depth. Check out Apparent Stoic for additional articles and practical suggestions for tranquility and Stoic parenting.
- **The Stoic Mom (www.thestoicmom.com).** Meredith Kunz discusses Stoic parenting, raising strong girls, and the usefulness of Stoicism for women. Her site addresses issues with older teens and tweens, including dealing with technology and peer pressure.

Finally, if you are eager to connect with other people interested in Stoicism, you can meet people online and in real life. Here are a few places to find them:

- **Stoic Parents Facebook group.** As the modern Stoic movement has grown, Stoics from all over the world have connected with one another on social media. You can easily use the search function on Facebook to find different groups related to Stoicism. The main one I recommend is Stoic Parents, where we help one another deal with parenting challenges using Stoic principles. We also try to encourage and inspire one another to apply Stoic ideals to everyday life with our children. There are many other general-interest Facebook groups as well, including Stoicism groups, Applying Stoicism, and Stoic Psychology.
- **Local Stoic groups.** The Stoic Fellowship website (www.stoicfellowship.com/home) has information on local in-person groups around the world. Groups have formed in many cities, so if you are interested, you might be able to join like-minded people for discussions. The group also has resources for starting your own Stoic group if one does not already exist in your area.
- **Stoic Week and Stoic Mindfulness and Resilience Training (SMRT).** The team behind Modern Stoicism also conducts two annual weeklong events on Stoicism. These are free and available at https://learn.modernstoicism.com. By participating in Stoic Week or SMRT, you can learn more, deepen your practice of Stoic principles, and connect with participants from across the globe.

I'm so glad you decided to pick up this book. I truly hope you have found it useful as a person and as a parent. Stoicism made my life better, and I believe it can make yours better too. If you aren't sure what steps to take next, I encourage you to connect with other people who are interested in Stoic parenting. The resources above should help you get started. Just remember, other parents are going through the same things you are, and we can help one another. Reach out, keep things in perspective, and don't feel guilty. With patience and persistence, you will find a way to become a calm, mindful, and engaged parent.

NOTES

INTRODUCTION

1. Children's names are pseudonyms.
2. William Irvine, *A Guide to the Good Life: The Ancient Art of Stoic Joy* (New York: Oxford University Press, 2009).
3. Donald Robertson, *Stoicism and the Art of Happiness* (London: Hodder & Stoughton, 2013).
4. Ryan Holiday and Stephen Hanselman, *The Daily Stoic: 366 Meditations on Wisdom, Perseverance, and the Art of Living* (New York: Portfolio, 2016).

I. DEVELOPING A PARENTING PHILOSOPHY

1. William Irvine, *A Guide to the Good Life: The Ancient Art of Stoic Joy* (New York: Oxford University Press, 2009), 1.
2. Massimo Pigliucci, *How to Be a Stoic: Using Ancient Philosophy to Live a Modern Life* (New York: Basic Books, 2017).
3. Christopher Gill, "What Is Stoic Virtue?" in *Stoicism Today: Selected Writings II*, ed. Patrick Ussher (self-pub., Stoicism Today, 2016), 15.
4. Ibid.
5. Ibid.

2. FOCUSING ON WHAT YOU
CAN CONTROL

1. Epictetus, *Handbook*, 1.1.

2. William Irvine, *A Guide to the Good Life: The Ancient Art of Stoic Joy* (New York: Oxford University Press, 2009), 89.

3. Ibid.

4. Ibid., 95.

3. RETHINKING YOUR VALUE JUDGMENTS

1. This is my own interpretation of the process based on two modern sources: Donald Robertson, *Stoicism and the Art of Happiness* (London: Hodder & Stoughton, 2013), 172–73; and John Sellars, *The Art of Living: The Stoics on the Nature and Function of Philosophy* (London: Bristol Classical Press, 2009), 157.

2. Epictetus, *Handbook*, 5.1.

3. Marcus Aurelius, *Meditations*, 8.49.

4. Robertson, *Stoicism and the Art of Happiness*, 175–77.

5. Marcus Aurelius, *Meditations*, 6.13.

6. Marcus Aurelius, *Meditations*, 8.48.

7. For a similar technique, see Robertson's Leaves on a Stream meditation in Robertson, *Stoicism and the Art of Happiness*, 182–83.

4. ENGAGING WITH OTHER PEOPLE

1. See Massimo Pigliucci, *How to Be a Stoic: Using Ancient Philosophy to Live a Modern Life* (New York: Basic Books, 2017), chapter 8, for a full discussion of this concept.

2. Epictetus, *Discourses*, 2.26, 1–2.

3. Epictetus, *Discourses*, 2.26, 4–5.

4. Marcus Aurelius, *Meditations*, 2.1.

5. Marcus Aurelius, *Meditations*, 10.4.

6. Marcus Aurelius, *Meditations*, 8.59.

7. Marcus Aurelius, *Meditations*, 11.18.

8. Marcus Aurelius, *Meditations*, 2.1.

9. Marcus Aurelius, *Meditations*, 11.18.

5. TEACHING YOUR CHILD VIRTUE

1. A. A. Long, *Epictetus: A Stoic and Socratic Guide to Life* (Oxford: Oxford University Press, 2002), 193.
2. Gaius Musonius Rufus, *Lectures and Sayings*, Lecture 4.7.
3. Ibid.
4. Seneca, *Selected Letters*, Letters 95.40 and 95.44.
5. Seneca, *Selected Letters*, Letter 95.12.

6. ENJOYING YOUR CHILD

1. Donald Robertson, *Stoicism and the Art of Happiness* (London: Hodder & Stoughton, 2013), 191.
2. William Irvine, *A Guide to the Good Life: The Ancient Art of Stoic Joy* (New York: Oxford University Press, 2009), 79.
3. Epictetus, *Handbook*, 26.
4. Irvine, *A Guide to the Good Life*, 68.
5. Ibid., 106–7.
6. Robertson, *Stoicism and the Art of Happiness*, 223.
7. Marcus Aurelius, *Meditations*, 7.48–49.
8. Seneca, *Dialogues and Essays*, 3.36.
9. Robertson, *Stoicism and the Art of Happiness*, 203–9.
10. Ibid., 205.
11. Meditation techniques in this chapter are adapted from ibid., 203–9.
12. Seneca, *Dialogues and Essays*, 3.36.
13. Ibid.

7. OVERCOMING YOUR ANXIETY

1. Visit the American Psychiatric Association webpage for more information about mental illness: https://www.psychiatry.org/patients-families.
2. Marcus Aurelius, *Meditations*, 8.49.
3. This is my own interpretation of the process based on two modern sources: Donald Robertson, *Stoicism and the Art of Happiness* (London: Hodder & Stoughton, 2013), 172–73; and John Sellars, *The Art of Living: The Stoics on the Nature and Function of Philosophy* (London: Bristol Classical Press, 2009), 157.

4. William Irvine, *A Guide to the Good Life: The Ancient Art of Stoic Joy* (New York: Oxford University Press, 2009), 80.

5. Ibid., 89.

6. See Robertson, *Stoicism and the Art of Happiness*, 112–18, for a discussion of how Stoics rely on role models.

7. Ibid., 197.

8. Epictetus, *Discourses*, 2.18, 25.

9. Ibid.

10. Epictetus, *Discourses*, 2.18, 23.

11. Epictetus, *Discourses*, 2.18, 27–28.

8. FINDING TRANQUILITY

1. Margaret R. Graver, *Stoicism and Emotion* (Chicago: University of Chicago Press, 2007), 58.

2. Seneca, *Selected Letters*, Letter 59.14.

3. Epictetus, *Discourses*, 1.23, 5.

4. Donald Robertson, *Stoicism and the Art of Happiness* (London: Hodder & Stoughton, 2013), 100.

5. Gaius Musonius Rufus, *Lectures and Sayings*, Lecture 3.4.

6. Epictetus, *Discourses*, 2.22.

7. Robertson, *Stoicism and the Art of Happiness*, 103.

8. Seneca, *Selected Letters*, Letter 72.4.

9. Robertson, *Stoicism and the Art of Happiness*, 104.

10. Epictetus, *Discourses*, 1.25, 7–8.

BIBLIOGRAPHY

Epictetus. *Discourses, Fragments, Handbook*. Translated by Robin Hard. Oxford: Oxford University Press, 2014.

Gaius Musonius Rufus. *Lectures and Sayings*. Translated by Cynthia King. William B. Irvine, CreateSpace, 2011.

Gill, Christopher. "What Is Stoic Virtue?" In *Stoicism Today: Selected Writings II*, edited by Patrick Ussher, 15. Self-published, Stoicism Today, 2016.

Graver, Margaret R. *Stoicism and Emotion*. Chicago: University of Chicago Press, 2007.

Holiday, Ryan, and Stephen Hanselman. *The Daily Stoic: 366 Meditations on Wisdom, Perseverance, and the Art of Living*. New York: Portfolio, 2016.

Irvine, William. *A Guide to the Good Life: The Ancient Art of Stoic Joy*. New York: Oxford University Press, 2009.

Long, A. A. *Epictetus: A Stoic and Socratic Guide to Life*. Oxford: Oxford University Press, 2002.

Marcus Aurelius. *Meditations*. Translated by Robin Hard. New York: Oxford University Press, 2011.

Pigliucci, Massimo. *How to Be a Stoic: Using Ancient Philosophy to Live a Modern Life*. New York: Basic Books, 2017.

Robertson, Donald. *Stoicism and the Art of Happiness*. London: Hodder & Stoughton, 2013.

Sellars, John. *The Art of Living: The Stoics on the Nature and Function of Philosophy*. London: Bristol Classical Press, 2009.

Seneca. "On Anger, Book 3." In *Dialogues and Essays*. Translated by John Davie. New York: Oxford University Press, 2008.

———. *Selected Letters*. Translated by Elaine Fantham. New York: Oxford University Press, 2010.

ACKNOWLEDGMENTS

I would like to thank the scholars whose work I draw on heavily in this book and the members of the Modern Stoicism team, for helping bring Stoicism back to life. This book would not have been possible without their insights and dedication. I am grateful for the continued support of my parents, Keith and Pam Bryant, and my siblings, Corley Bryant, Lexie Bryant, and Lenora Bryant. And most of all, I am thankful (every day) for the love and support of my husband, Ali Polat. You're the one who made it happen. Thanks for everything.

INDEX

ABOUT THE AUTHOR

Brittany Polat is a practicing Stoic, mother to three young children, and blogger who writes about Stoic family life. She is especially interested in exploring ways that Stoic principles can lead to a rich and rewarding life for parents and children. See more of her writing on her blog at apparentstoic.com.